ignite

ignite

HOW TO SPARK IMMEDIATE GROWTH
IN YOUR CHURCH

nelson searcy

WITH JENNIFER DYKES HENSON

BakerBooks

a division of Baker Publishing Group
Grand Rapids, Michigan

© 2009 by Nelson Searcy

Published by Baker Books
a division of Baker Publishing Group
P.O. Box 6287, Grand Rapids, MI 49516-6287
www.bakerbooks.com

Printed in the United States of America

Library of Congress Cataloging-in-Publication Data
Searcy, Nelson.
    Ignite : how to spark immediate growth in your church / Nelson Searcy ; with Jennifer Dykes Henson.
       p.   cm.
    ISBN 978-0-8010-7216-1 (pbk.)
       1. Church growth. I. Henson, Jennifer Dykes. II. Title.
    BV652.25.S43 2009
    254'.5—dc22   2009023291

To my son, Alexander Searcy: I love you very much. At the time of this writing, you are too young to know Jesus Christ personally, even though you are covered by his grace and I love to hear you pray, but I pray that as you mature you will place your faith and trust in Jesus at the earliest possible moment. No decision you make will be as important as this one. I pray for you every day.

contents

acknowledgments

Within hours of becoming a Christian, I became passionate about evangelism. This book is one expression of
that passion. My eternal gratitude is to Jesus Christ for calling
me to salvation and later to ministry. While dozens if not hundreds of pastors have influenced my thinking on evangelism,
two stand above the rest: Milton A. Hollifield, Jr., and Rick
Warren. Thank you both for taking a chance on me when I was
either way too young or way too inexperienced to accomplish
the ministry assignments you gave me.

In addition I would like to especially thank the following
pastors and church leaders for influencing my views and shap-
ing my thoughts on church growth: Donald McGavran, Peter
Wagner, Win and Charles Arn, Thom Rainer, Billy Graham,
George Hunter, Carl George, and DeLos Miles. If the theology
and applications in this book are correct, you can thank the
pastors above. If there are mistakes, those are solely mine.

I must also express a huge thanks to my colleagues at The Journey Church, both past and present staff members. Since 2001 I have had the privilege of being the dumbest person on an extremely smart team. Kerrick Thomas, Jason Hatley, Sarah Wilson, and John Troy have especially shaped the thoughts in this book. To the current staff: I love doing church with you! To future staff: what are you waiting on? Step up to the plate and join me in the adventure of cooperating with God to influence New York City toward Jesus!

This is my first book with Baker but I hope not my last. My thanks to Chad Allen, Jack Kuhatschek, and all the fine folks at Baker Books who have made this book infinitely stronger than it was when I submitted the original manuscript. I must also acknowledge Bucky Rosenbaum of the Rosenbaum Agency for his early counsel in making this project possible.

Jennifer Dykes Henson has been a partner on my last four books. Her skills as a writer and editor are hard to overstate. I cannot say thank you enough! As members at The Journey, Jennifer and her husband Brian serve as models of all that I discuss in this book.

My sincere thanks to the coaching alumni who share their testimonies in this book. You help bring the principles alive and are a model for all who read this book.

Finally, I must thank the love of my life, Kelley. I'm glad you showed up for our blind date back in 1992 (and our wedding date in 1994). Each day my love for you grows stronger. Thank you for your commitment to this book and your continual support. Alexander is lucky to have a mom like you, and I'm proud to call you my wife.

Jennifer Dykes Henson—To my brother, Jimmy: thank you for the seeds of love and support you have sown into my life and for your constant example of evangelism's true heart. And to my grandfather, Joseph Edward Reeves: thank you for the legacy you ignited.

introduction

What If Your Church
Could Double in One Day?

Jon and Liz got married right out of college. They were just kids, really, but they were in love. They couldn't wait to start life.

After the wedding, they bought a two-story home on the edge of town and leased a nicer car than either one of them had ever driven. Jon got a job as an assistant to the president of a local bank, and Liz went to work as a photographer, taking pictures for the community newspaper. Three years later, their daughter, Madison, made her debut. Then, a year and a half later, their son, Johnny, came along.

Jon and Liz looked like they had it made. They were living the dream. And they were happy . . . most of the time. Sure, they had their share of fits and fights, just like anyone else. And

Jon did get a little overwhelmed trying to make ends meet each month. But that was normal, right?

They even went to church from time to time. Well, early on in their marriage they did. They hadn't been in a few years now. The weekends seemed to fly by, and Jon didn't see any real benefit in getting dressed up and spending his Sunday mornings in a pew. Liz mentioned wanting to go back every once in a while, but there always seemed to be a reason to put it off. Now that the kids were getting older, though, she thought about it more and more. She just didn't know how to convince Jon. It wasn't worth the fight.

But recently Jon had mentioned a guy in his office, Sam, who kept inviting him to go to a new church in town called FCC (Fictional Community Church). Jon didn't seem interested. Liz was kind of hoping—okay, even praying—that he would change his mind.

Dream with me for a moment. Let the following question roll around in your mind:

What if your church could double in one day?

I often tell my congregation that we can easily double on any given Sunday as long as one thing happens: everyone invites an unchurched friend! Just think about that. Your church could double next Sunday if everyone in your congregation got on board. You could immediately double your evangelistic effectiveness if everyone invited one unchurched friend to church.

The real conundrum about a church doubling in a day isn't how we do it but why it isn't happening every Sunday. Why is it that my church and your church can go months (or even years) without significant growth? Do we think that's what God wants? What if we could ignite an evangelistic revolution where evangelism happens every Sunday and churches double every year? That's what this book is all about.

Over the next thirteen chapters, I will show you how you can:

- create a consistent culture of evangelism in your church, one where you see new people coming to faith in Jesus week after week
- raise the evangelistic temperature of your church and keep it boiling hot
- mobilize your people to influence their unchurched friends for Jesus Christ and his church
- create awareness of your church in the community so that when God's Spirit prompts someone to attend church, your church comes to mind
- increase the number of first-time unchurched guests who attend your church (this book is actually a prequel to my book *Fusion: Turning First-Time Guests to Fully-Engaged Members of Your Church*)
- prepare for new believers and partner with God in seeing more people than ever come to faith in Jesus

In other words, I want to give you a clear system for cooperating with God to see consistent, high-impact, Christ-honoring evangelistic fruit in your church; a practical, nuts-and-bolts process for developing an effective evangelism system. But first I must address a couple of evangelism truths.

Evangelism Truth One: God Wants Lost People Found More Than You Do

I have a friend who owns an art gallery. He tells me that there is a correlation between someone's desire for a piece of art and the price that person is willing to pay. If someone really wants something from his gallery, they are willing to pay an exorbitantly high price. In fact, his clients often get in intense bidding wars over a coveted piece.

We can see how much God desires for us to be reconciled to him by how much he was willing to pay. He paid the highest price possible! The most famous verse in the Bible reminds us how much God was willing to pay for his creation, his own work of art:

> For God loved the world so much that he gave his one and only Son, so that everyone who believes in him will not perish but have eternal life.
>
> John 3:16

You are no doubt reading this book because you care about sharing that truth with the people in your community—the people God has paid for but has not been able to receive. As much as you want to see the unchurched come to faith in Jesus and become a part of God's family, he wants it even more.

Ignite is not just about church growth or church systems (my area of specialty). This is ultimately a book that will help you align your church with the heart of God. A church that is effective in evangelism is a church that is in step with God's purposes, connected to God's heart, and blessed by God's power.

I like to refer to evangelism as "attracting a crowd to worship." In other words, it's the process of moving someone from the community to the crowd so that they can ultimately be moved into the congregation and then the core. You may be familiar with the concept of "Circles of Commitment" from Rick Warren's classic textbook *The Purpose-Driven Church*. These circles define the levels a person moves through from the time they are introduced to the church to the time they become a fully developing follower of Jesus. Warren contends, and I concur, that the goal of a living, growing church is to "move people from the outer circle (low commitment/low spiritual maturity) to the inner circle (high commitment/high spiritual maturity),"[1] as represented by the concentric circles:

God desires to see the unchurched in your community move toward faith in Jesus Christ.

While the heart of evangelism is the desire to move people from the community to the core, the evangelism system outlined in this book will focus on bringing people from the community into the crowd. When this system is used side by side with the assimilation system found in *Fusion: Turning First-Time Guests into Fully-Engaged Members of Your Church*, you will have a practical plan for moving people all the way through the process. More importantly, you will have a plan for doing your part to give people the best possible opportunity to become fully developing followers of Jesus Christ.

Let's add to the circles one of my favorite definitions of evangelism. It comes from the Anglican Archbishop's Committee on Evangelism back in 1918 and has since been modified by the Lausanne Committee for World Evangelisation. This definition states that "to evangelize is to so present Christ Jesus, in the power of the Holy Spirit, that men shall come to put their trust in God through Him, to accept Him as their Savior, serve him as their King in the fellowship of His church."[2] Now that is a solid definition.

At our church, The Journey, we've molded this definition to fit our time and culture. In our words, "to evangelize is to invite others through the power of the Holy Spirit to put their trust in God through Jesus Christ, to accept Jesus as their Savior and follow Him as their leader in everyday life as members of a local church." Couple this with my earlier assertion that evangelism is attracting a crowd to worship, and you have a full understanding of what it means to evangelize.

Evangelism Truth Two: Evangelism Is a Both-And Proposition, Not Either-Or

Effective evangelism happens when a church embraces what has been called "the genius of the and."[3] People have a hard time with this concept because we are wired to love either-or propositions. We love choosing a side, taking a stance. Many of our cultural systems thrive on either-or thinking. In your own life, you are either a Republican or a Democrat. Your favorite color is red or blue or green, not rainbow. You embrace the private school system or the public school system. You watch MSNBC or Fox News. You root for the Yankees or the Mets (are there any other teams?).

Unfortunately, this either-or thinking sometimes creeps into the church, especially in the area of evangelism. Many churches I've worked with like to define their evangelism strategy as either *this* or *that*. In broad terms, the choice is to embrace either "come see evangelism" or "go tell evangelism."

"Come see evangelism" might be thought of as event evangelism, marketing/promotion evangelism, entertainment evangelism, attractional evangelism, or, dare I say, seeker evangelism. Strategies for this type of evangelism can be quite effective, as we'll be discussing. On the other side of the coin, "go tell evangelism" is often thought of as personal evangelism, incarnational evangelism, friendship evangelism, or missional living. Strategies for this type of evangelism can also be extremely effective. Amazingly enough, the two don't have to volley against each other. They work together very well. In this book I will not propose that you use either "come see evangelism" or "go tell evangelism." I will propose that you use both, just as Jesus did. If you only use one or the other, then your evangelism system will be, at best, half as effective as it could be.

Before we jump in, let me give you a few guidelines for preparing to achieve your evangelism goals:

1. *Read and digest this book.* Grab a highlighter or pen and work your way through the following pages. I am going to outline a system for evangelizing your community and keeping the fruits of your labor—one that has been proven by time and experience. Make notes in the margins, disagree with me, laugh at me, or raise your eyebrows. I don't mind. All I ask is that you move through the information thoroughly and with a heart toward what God wants to accomplish as a result of your evangelistic outreach.

2. *Study this book with others on your staff or in your church.* Any successful evangelism system will require the commitment of dozens, if not hundreds, of people. Through this book, you and your staff can learn how to work together to mobilize your people for evangelism. By studying the book together, you will be better able to build constructive discussion around the principles I'll be presenting.

3. *Be open to new ideas.* Some of what is presented here goes against traditional thinking on evangelism. If you run into an idea that is contrary to what you've been exposed to, that's okay. Stay open. Don't let discomfort close your mind. The information presented here is not theory; it is the result of a lot of trial and error, flights and crashes, and some God-sized successes that surprised us. I may challenge familiar concepts but never scriptural essentials.

Peter tells us, "The Lord isn't really being slow about his promise, as some people think. No, he is being patient for your sake. He does not want anyone to be destroyed, but wants everyone to repent" (2 Peter 3:9). God wants the people in your community to know him, and he has handpicked you to evangelize them. The system I am about to detail has proven effective in growing churches and helping people across the world to take unhindered steps toward knowing Jesus. I am excited to share it with you.

Now that we've laid the foundation, let's get started by looking at how a "big day" can jump-start evangelism in your church.

Church Leader Testimony

From understanding my role in evangelism as the pastor of the church to understanding how to create an environment that promotes personal evangelism and learning how to be strategic by understanding when people are most open and receptive to the gospel, the evangelism system training has equipped not only me but my entire church of over six hundred weekly to reach others for Jesus Christ. Without God and these valuable tools, we could not have been as effective in reaching others.

Bryan Gerstel, Lead Pastor
The Pointe United Methodist Church (Albany, GA)

1

what a difference a day makes

This Book's Big Idea

Those who believed what Peter said were baptized and added to the church that day—about 3,000 in all.

Acts 2:41

Each day let us follow more faithfully, more courageously, more daringly the lead of our great Captain who bids us follow Him.

William Thomson Hanzsche

You've had big days in your life. Think about the day you graduated from high school or college, the day you got married, or the day your first child was born. These are the days that change everything. They infuse a new spark into life. And they are not days that happen haphazardly, are they? No, they are days you plan for, prepare for, and eagerly look toward. You want to be ready when they get here, so you study hard and ace all of your exams; you buy a suit or a dress and send out invitations months in advance; you put furniture together and paint nursery walls. Why? So that when that big day comes you have everything in place. You are ready for it. You are positioned to fully receive the change it is going to bring into your life.

Have you had big days like these in the life of your church? Can you look back and pinpoint one or two days in the last couple of years that changed your course, helped you break through a barrier, or took you to the next level? Maybe you had a big Easter service last year that brought you a lot of first-timers. Or perhaps you did a special forty-day study that pulled in quite a few people from your community. Were you able to keep those new people? Were you positioned and ready for them? Did you capitalize on the momentum, or did it fizzle out as things slipped back to the status quo?

If we plan big days in our lives and those days have the potential to change everything for us, why can't we assume that the same truth would apply to our churches? Couldn't big days help us move toward where we want to be? Instead of just gearing up for important days and events haphazardly and seeing little to no lasting results, what if we put a system in place that would help us plan and execute all kinds of big days effectively—and help us keep the fruit we would see them bring? Think of it this way: What if there were two additional "Easter-level" days in your church every year? Could that help you grow? Could those days help you reach more of your community for Jesus?

The story of The Journey Church is best told through recalling a series of big days. In 2002 my wife Kelley and I launched

The Journey in New York City with—you guessed it—a big day. We planned our launch for Easter Sunday. Why? Because we knew Easter was a natural big day that we could cooperate with to gain some initial momentum. We spent months planning and preparing for the launch, and when the day finally arrived, 110 people showed up. That may not sound like a lot, but for a new church in the middle of Manhattan, it's a great turnout. I was thrilled. But I quickly learned my first church growth principle: not everyone who shows up at your church on Easter shows up again the next week. Over the next few months, I grew The Journey down to thirty-five people.

If you've been in ministry for any time at all, you know that growth barriers are very real and very tough to break. I have found that most churches face growth barriers at 65, 125, 250, 500, 1000, and 2500. Obviously, at this point in the Journey's story, I was struggling just to make it back past 65. As the concept of the big day continued to develop for me, I began to realize that I could create and take advantage of other big days—like that first Easter Sunday—to break through and gain momentum. So my team and I planned a new series and decided to kick it off with a big day. We broke through the 65 growth barrier. The next year, we planned three big days—and broke 125. Eventually big days helped us break 250, 500, and 1000.

The big day is a proven process that has helped us reach more people for Jesus Christ. We've seen it help churches across the country as well. In working with pastors and church leaders from coast to coast, we have watched churches running 65–70 break 100 through a big day, churches running 360–380 break 500 through a big day, and churches running 700–800 break 1000. So think about what's possible in your church. What could

God do in one day if you cooperated with him to reach as many people in your community as possible?

A Big Day

Before we go any further, let's define what a big day is:

> A big day is an all-out push toward a single Sunday for the purpose of breaking the next growth barrier and setting an attendance record in order to reach as many people as possible for Jesus.

Some of you may get stuck on the "attendance record" part of that definition. Let me assure you, the attendance record that you want to set through a big day has nothing to do with earning bragging rights among your pastor friends. It's all about making sure you create a level of excitement that will bring in a bigger number of people than ever before so that lives can be changed and your church can become even more of a thriving force in your community.

When you do an all-out push toward a big day, something begins to change in the life of your church. People get excited. The community starts to buzz. God blesses the effort you are putting in. And why wouldn't he? After all, big days are his idea. I didn't create this big day concept. God did. A brief look back through history clearly shows how God has used big days as part of his plan since the beginning of time. In fact, time began with a big day. Wouldn't you agree that it was a big day when God divided the light from the darkness and brought the world into existence? He had probably been planning the details of that day for a while. And if you study your Old Testament, you'll find many more big days that God used to advance his purposes.

Perhaps one of the most famous and relevant of God's big days—this one in the New Testament—was the day of Pentecost. That's the day Peter preached and three thousand were saved. God used that one big day to rapidly expand the church. This should lead us to consider the question, "How fast can the church grow?" If we use the day of Pentecost as our measuring stick, we shouldn't see doubling in a day as that big of a deal. God took the church from a handful of followers to thousands in one day, and yet we doubt his ability to do the same in our churches. Why is that?

God is the same yesterday, today, and tomorrow. The God who engineered the day of Pentecost is the same God to whom you are entrusting your church. Is it possible that he would do something like that again, if we were willing to cooperate? I believe that it is. Your church may not go from a handful to over three thousand on one Sunday (or maybe it will), but by understanding and working with the power of a big day, you can tap into what God wants to do through the church in our day and see some amazing things happen. (For more on big days in the book of Acts, keep reading—more to come on page 39.)

Deciding to harness the potential of big days is simply agreeing to cooperate with God's plan, in accordance with the way he has worked—and will continue to work—throughout history. We already know of another big day that God has in store. Just study the book of Revelation. Until that day when God's plan for salvation is ultimately fulfilled, we have the opportunity to work with him to reach as many people as possible for the sake of Jesus Christ. That's what the big day is all about.

Why a Big Day?

Planning and executing a big day is not an easy task. It takes a lot of work. So when you are deep in the trenches and expenses of pulling the details together, you had better understand why you are doing it. Perspective is everything. If your "why" is big enough, you can deal with almost any "what." So why should you worry about pushing past your next growth barrier? Why do a big day? Consider these four reasons:

1. Do a Big Day to Reach New People

As we just discussed, the biggest reason to do a big day is to cooperate with God in reaching the most people possible for the kingdom while we still can. That's the big picture. But let's bring that down to where we live every day. Stop for a minute and think about the city or town that is buzzing just outside your door. People are dying every day—dying small daily deaths of frustration, fear, addiction, and depression and dying physical deaths that will separate them from God eternally.

We have a responsibility to do as much as we can to bring these dying people to Christ, point them to new life, and grow them up into spiritual maturity. Isn't that why we do what we do? But reaching our communities is not going to happen without some intentional effort on our part. We can't just walk through status quo days and assume that the people who are already in our churches are going to be filled with a passion to reach others for Jesus. We have to make a concerted decision to put time and energy into influencing those countless people beyond our doors. They need us. That's where the vision for a big day begins—with a heart for the community and a heart to reach new people before God's final big day.

On a side note, let me commend you for walking this path. Deciding to move through a growth barrier and reach a new level through a big day is a tremendous act of unselfishness. Can I be honest with you? It's all too easy for church leaders to stagnate. It's easy to hang out in the comfort zone, keep the bills paid, preach to the same crowd every week, and just let things roll on. But that is selfish. When you land in that place, what you are saying to the community around you is, "I don't care about you. I am comfortable with things just as they are." The truth is, who is going to touch the people in your area if not you?

To get serious about doing a big day means breaking out of selfish strongholds. It means realizing that church is not about you and yours but rather about God's purpose for the people you've been called to reach. We all know that Jesus said, "Therefore, go and make disciples of all the nations, baptizing them in the name of the Father and the Son and the Holy Spirit. Teach these new disciples to obey all the commands I have given you" (Matt. 28:19–20). Why then is it so easy for us to get caught in maintenance mode and leave that commission to someone else? By investing your time in learning to ignite your church for healthy growth, you are choosing to unselfishly follow the calling. Thank you for that.

2. Do a Big Day to Make the Devil Mad

Okay, this shouldn't be anyone's primary reason for doing a big day, but every once in a while it's good to do something that will irk Satan. If he's not bothered by what you are doing, you must not be doing much against his cause. Or as a pastor and mentor of mine once advised me, "If you haven't met the devil head-on lately, maybe it's because you are moving in the same direction!"

You'll find, though, that the devil is not the only one who gets mad when you start to spend time and energy on reaching new people. The unfortunate truth is that some people in your church will get mad too. Those who are comfortable with the present reality and don't want to be bothered with a pesky thing like evangelism probably won't like the idea of a big day. They don't want their pew to get too full. They don't want their parking place to be taken by someone else. You need to prepare yourself. Satan will use some of these people to try to discourage you and pull you away from God's purposes.

God's kingdom has never been and will never be built on the foundation of complacency. When you get serious about evangelism, you will force some of the complacent Christians in your church to reconsider their membership. Inwardly focused Christians don't mesh well with outwardly focused churches. They will either leave or get back in alignment with God's plan for their spiritual growth. Thankfully, our God works all things together for good. If complacent Christians choose to leave, that's the kind of subtraction that paves the way for greater addition. Think of it as separating the grain from the chaff.

Here's a question for you to consider: what could you do over the next twelve months, in addition to a big day, that would make the devil mad and reach the unchurched? Several years ago I pulled our staff together for a memorable brainstorming session where I asked: "What is the riskiest thing we can do to reach people? What would really make the devil mad?" The answer we came up with was rather unusual: advertise on *The Howard Stern Show*. At that time *The Howard Stern Show* was the most influential radio show in our city. So we decided we would use Stern's position and prominence with our demographic to reach an unchurched audience with an invitation to our next big day—the kickoff of our February teaching series. We made the devil and quite a few complacent Christians from other churches mad. But we reached a ton of unchurched people through that series.

3. Do a Big Day to Grow the Christians in Your Church

The people in your church would love to be passionate about evangelism, whether they realize it yet or not. People need a cause. They like to be stirred and long to be a part of something that is bigger than they are. They don't want to check a box of church attendance and leave it there. No, they want to know that their life, and their service, really matters. Reminding them of the importance of evangelism by planning a big day gets them excited about cooperating with God to grow the church and makes them want to do their part to help.

There's nothing like a big day to ignite some passion and mobilize people for service. When you share your vision for reaching a new level through a big day, you will find people more than willing to give extra time and energy to the cause. They will help prepare the way for that big day, and they will be there to take part in it. They will be eager to reach out to their friends, family, and co-workers. You will spur them on to greater spiritual growth by giving them the opportunity to be part of the bigger picture of growing God's kingdom.

4. Do a Big Day to Build Momentum in Your Church

I run into a lot of churches who say, "We feel like our momentum is beginning to wane." If you can relate, that's all the more reason to do a big day. Big days build momentum on many levels. First of all, they involve your people in working toward a big push, as I mentioned. That on its own will generate momentum. Second, planning your big day can attract attention from the community. People are drawn to a big event. If they hear about a church that's planning to do something exciting and fresh, they will talk about it—and, very likely, they will show up to see it happen.

Lastly, a big day builds momentum by propelling you to the next level of growth. If you follow the pre– and post–big day system that will be outlined in these pages, your church will still be significantly bigger three months after the big day than it was before. And then it will be significantly bigger three months after your next big day than it was before that one. See how it works? As you reach more people, you plug more people in to become fully developing followers of Jesus, which gives you the incentive and ability to continue reaching more people . . . and the spiral toward heaven continues.

Church Leader Testimony

At Peckville Assembly of God, we've found that big days are one of the best ways of reaching people for Christ and building his church. We've learned that people need a specific reason to invite their friends to church.

Terry Drost, Lead Pastor
Peckville Assembly of God (Blakely, PA)

2

what day is it?

Surveying the Options

For everything there is a season, a time for every activity under heaven.

Ecclesiastes 3:1

Why always, "not yet"? Do the flowers in the spring say "not yet"?

Norman Douglas

Back to those important days in your life. How did you choose them? Granted, you probably couldn't choose your graduation day or the day of your child's birth (just as you can't choose the date for Easter Sunday), but you can choose some of your big days. Your wedding day is a great example. How did you, or how will you, decide on that date? Not haphazardly, I'm sure.

You probably factored in how long the wedding would take to plan, what would be most convenient for your family and friends, your favorite season of the year, and the list goes on and on. You want your wedding day to go off without a hitch (couldn't resist), so countless factors go into planning it for the most opportune time. The same is true with your church's big day.

Save the Date

Once you decide to do a big day, the next step is to pick the most strategic date for that big day. I don't suggest that you decide on the day by throwing darts at a calendar. The date you choose is extremely important—more important than you may think—and many factors play into scheduling it in a way that will bring you the best results. Just as certain times of the year are more suited than others for weddings (almost half of all weddings take place within a four-week period), certain times of the year are more suited for a big day. Let's look at three of the best big day opportunities.

1. Easter Sunday—The Built-In Big Day

Easter is a big day "gimme." God has already put this one on the calendar for you, so your job is to make sure you treat it like the big day it is. The tricky thing about Easter is that it falls on a different Sunday every year. You have to keep in mind that the unchurched aren't really thinking about the fact that Easter is approaching. Even though a lot of families who don't normally go to church will plan to show up on Easter, it's not a set date on their calendars like Christmas is. So you have to work a little harder to get them to show up.

Deciding to use Easter as a big day gives you the opportunity to maximize the increased turnout you are already destined to have. If you've never done a big day, this is a great one to start with because a large part of the structure is already in place. An Easter big day can be especially effective on the years that it falls early, giving you plenty of time to connect people into the church before they start scattering for summer vacations. You have time to get them involved on a deeper level before the summer slump. On the flip side, a late Easter is still a great big day. All you have to do is maximize it for growth, which we will talk more about a little later. For now, go ahead and mark this coming Easter as a big day on your calendar. (For a free report on "How to Maximize Easter" as a big day in your church, visit www.ignitebook.com.)

2. Fall—The Back-to-School Big Day

Fall is one of the best times of the year for a big day, and the best time in the fall for your big day is one month after school begins. Yes, you read correctly—you should schedule your big day for approximately one month *after* school begins. People often ask me, "Why not have the big day right as school begins? You know, kick everything off together?" This seems like a logical thing to do, but it doesn't work out so well in reality. First of all, your regular attenders and members won't start returning to church with normalcy until the Sunday after school begins. You need some time for them to get back in the swing of things before your big day. You need to be able to cast vision for the fall and get them on board with the push for outreach. This month is your momentum-building period.

Second, at The Journey and with other churches I've worked with, I've found that reaching unchurched people is even more difficult than usual for the first couple of weeks after school starts. Church is not on their radar. They are consumed with getting everyone back in a routine, getting to soccer practice and ballet class, getting homework done, and so on. Since church is not already a priority in their lives, this is not the time to push the issue. Give them a month to settle into the school year and get back on track. Then they'll be more ready to accept your invitation to attend a big day.

Check with your school system to see when school starts, and then plan accordingly. Keep in mind that you don't want to do your big day on Labor Day weekend. People will be trying to get in one more quick trip to the beach or lake. Attendance is usually down. And don't plan for the weekend after Labor Day either. The Sunday before your big day is an important time for mobilizing your congregation by casting some clear vision for the months to come. So depending on how your community's school calendar falls, you may need to plan your big day for as much as five or six weeks after school starts.

3. February—The Unexpected Big Day

You may be surprised by this, but February is an extremely effective time to do a big day. It's a hidden gem of a month that you can maximize to help you break through growth barriers. Why? First of all, people stay local in February. No one is traveling; they're hibernating. It's cold outside. Everyone is living modestly, trying to pay off the Christmas bills. Not much is in the hopper to compete with your big day.

Second, February brings with it a host of emotional needs that stay repressed during other months. The days are short. It's dark. In a lot of households, this leads to tension and fighting. Despite (or maybe because of) Valentine's Day, many people face serious relationship problems in February. These realities give the church a perfect opportunity to step up and say, "Hey, we know things are tough. We have an answer to what's going on in your life." If you plan a sermon series around the evident felt needs of the month, people will be eager to hear what you have to say. I'll talk more about planning your preaching to complement your big day in chapter 5.

February is also an ideal time for a big day because of its proximity to Easter. If you have a big day in mid-February, you will usually have five to eight weeks before Easter. That double boom of two big days close together is a great way to build fast momentum and break through some barriers. Imagine that you have a February big day that brings a record number of people to your church. As you follow up with those newcomers and help them get plugged in, you will be in the throes of planning for Easter—a big day that they will be excited to take part in. They will want to serve. They'll be more willing than many longtime Christians to talk to their friends about coming to church. The momentum that will occur as you build up to Easter will help you solidify the connection of these new attenders with your church.

4. Your Pick—The Big Day of Choice

To fill in any seeming dry spells in your annual calendar, I suggest that you pick one more day each year and make it a big day. This big day probably won't be as big as your Easter, fall, and February big days—because it won't necessarily have the natural rhythm of the calendar supporting it—but it can give you another burst of momentum at what you consider a low time. To balance out The Journey's annual calendar, I usually create a big day in the summer. I will either kick off a big summer sermon series or leverage an existing day, like Father's Day, and turn it into a reason for people to invite their friends. One of my coaching alumni created a big day around Father's Day by doing a special barbecue for men after the services and giving away a gas grill that any man would be proud to have on his patio. Be creative, but don't overdo it.

Church Leader Testimony

We have been doing big days for years with measurable success. In the weeks leading up to our last big day, we averaged 388 people per week. Our big day attendance was 642. Since that big day, we are averaging 476 people each week.

Clint Cook, Lead Pastor
Real Life Church (Springfield, IL)

Take a look at this chart, which shows how four big days over the course of a year could help a church of 180 in attendance break through the 250 barrier:

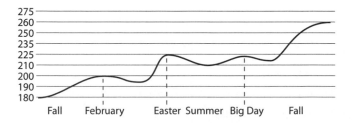

Big Days in the Early Church

A Brief History to Spur You toward Further Study

The early church gives us great examples of the power of big days:

The book of Acts begins with the "biggest" big day of all—Pentecost! On that one day, the church grew from 120 believers (see Acts 1:15) to over 3,000 (see Acts 2:41).

By Acts 4:4, the church had grown to at least 5,000 people, and by Acts 5:14 multitudes were being added to the church.

In Acts 6:7 we find that the church was increasing greatly and adding a large number of priests.

Acts 8:5–25 tells of a big day in Samaria, when a revival broke out. After that we see similar events in Galilee, Lydda, Sharon, and Joppa (see Acts 9:31, 35, 42–43).

In Antioch, a city much like the city where I serve, a great many came to belief (see Acts 11:21, 24, 26).

The church also grew rapidly through big days outside of Palestine in places such as:

Antioch in Pisidia	Acts 13:14, 43–44, 48–49
Derbe	Acts 14:20–21
Galatia	Acts 16:6
Thessalonica	Acts 17:1, 4
Berea	Acts 17:10, 12
Corinth	Acts 18:8–11
Rome	Acts 28:14–16, 24, 30–31

By Acts 21:20 the church is growing so fast that it's impossible to calculate. James simply says that myriads were coming to faith (tens of thousands)!

Beyond the book of Acts, check out Ephesians 19:10; Romans 8:31; 15:19; 15:23.

For more on this expansion, see *A Theology of Church Growth* by George W. Peters and *Evangelism in the Early Church* by Michael Green.

Be strategic about scheduling your big day. Make sure it's a day that is going to give you the best opportunity to reach the most people possible in your community. When you plan in a way that honors God, he will give power to that plan. Once your date is set, you can move on to other aspects of working toward the day that has the potential to change the course of your church's history for all of eternity.

3

the day of harvest

The Importance of Prayer and Goals

Devote yourselves to prayer with an alert mind and a thankful heart.

Colossians 4:2

Pray as though everything depended on God. Work as though everything depended on you.

Saint Augustine

Once you've set the date for your big day, start covering the day—and the entire process leading up to the day—in prayer. While the prayer should begin with you, it is key to mobilize the prayers of others as well. Aim to get as many people praying for your big day as you possibly can. Be creative. How could you get everyone attending your church to start praying for the big day? Remember what Paul told the Corinthians about their banding together in prayer on his behalf: "On him we have set our hope that he will continue to deliver us, as you help us by your prayers. Then many will give thanks on our behalf for the *gracious favor granted us in answer to the prayers of many*" (2 Cor. 1:10–11 NIV, emphasis added).

At The Journey, we've done things like "24 Hours of Prayer," where someone is continually at the church (or at the church office) praying during the twenty-four hours before a big day. All of our attenders are invited to stop by and join in. We've also asked people to commit to praying ten minutes every day for the two weeks leading up to a big day. Sometimes my staff and I, along with any members or attenders who want to join in, will couple fasting with the prayer. Prayer and fasting for a big day will change the hearts of the people who are in your church before you even start your outreach to the unchurched.

Later in the New Testament, in Colossians 4:2–3, Paul teaches us, "Devote yourself to prayer with an alert mind and a thankful heart. Pray for us, too, that God will give us many opportunities to speak about his mysterious plan concerning Christ." We can learn a lot about mobilizing our people for prayer through this passage. First of all, if you give your people the challenge to pray for opportunities to invite people to church or to share their faith, God will open those doors for them. And he will make them aware of doors that are already open. Notice Paul's mention of "an alert mind." God may have already been giving your people opportunities for evangelism that they haven't been aware of. But as they begin to pray for such opportunities, their hearts will be drawn to what they are praying for and their eyes will be opened. When your members and regular attenders are praying this way, you will have already made huge strides toward evangelizing your community.

A Specific Prayer

"It is for us to pray not for tasks equal to our powers, but for powers equal to our tasks, to go forward with a great desire forever beating at the door of our hearts as we travel toward our distant goal." Any idea who is credited with this quotation? Let me give you a hint. She was both blind and deaf, yet in the face of her adversity, she never failed to understand the importance of and intricate balance between tasks, prayer, and goals. You guessed it: Helen Keller. She knew that one of the keys to great faith was to have tasks set before us—and goals in the distance—that would stretch us beyond our limits and cause us to rely on God's power.

As you begin to pray over your big day, make sure you set an attendance goal right up front. Yes, an attendance goal. Pinpoint a number. Now, I know that some will push back at the idea of goal setting within the church, but goals serve an important purpose. A goal will stretch you and at the same time give you a measuring stick to see just how far you've been stretched— or more aptly, to see how much God has done. One thing that many of us church leaders tend to forget is that God has goals for our churches, and his goals are much bigger than any we'll set for ourselves. He wants our churches to have a major impact on large numbers of people. Specific goals are simply statements of faith in what God wants to do.

The point of your big day, as we've already discussed, is to break through your growth barriers and set an attendance record in an effort to reach as many people as possible for Jesus. Don't you think you should consult God on how many people he would like to reach? If you don't set an attendance goal for your big day, how will you give him the glory for meeting and exceeding it? I guarantee that you will have a number in mind whether you set a prayerful goal or not. So make sure you seek God's direction on the issue. Ask him to show you what his goal for the day really is, and then ask him to accomplish that goal as only he can. By doing so, you are acknowledging that he is in control of your big day's outcome. You are releasing your plan for the day into his plan for the day.

When you follow God in setting an attendance goal, you propel momentum toward your big day in two major ways:

1. **Setting a goal builds anticipation.** Don't try to involve the whole church in setting your big day goals. That will just get you into a mess. But don't be a lone ranger either. If you are in a large church, sit down with your staff for a prayerful goal-setting session. If you are in a smaller church, consider involving the top 10 percent of your membership based on their active participation in your church. When you bring more people into the goal-setting process, it stokes excitement. God-sized goals stretch people's faith and make them eager to be fully committed to the big day.

2. **Setting a goal pushes you to become more than you are right now.** When you set an attendance goal for your big day, you immediately begin to think of the things you'll have to do to be prepared for that number of people. Maybe you have to start a second service. Maybe you

need to buy more first-timer gifts. Maybe you need to reexamine the way you do parking or run your volunteer ministry. The point is that once you have a goal in place, you can start working backward from it. You are in a position to say, "Okay, God, if that is your goal for our church, what do we have to become in order for that goal to be accomplished?"

If you aren't sure about goal setting, try thinking of it as a belief building exercise—because that's exactly what it is. When you prayerfully set a God-sized goal, God is the one who is going to accomplish it. You are putting your faith in him to do something that may seem virtually impossible to you. As you think toward your big day, nail down the answer to this question: "Do I want to use this day to accomplish my plans and my will for my church or God's plans and God's will?" I guarantee that God's will for your big day, and for your church on the whole, is bigger than you can hope or imagine. You can't reach those heights in your own power, but you can reach them in God's power, as he has already ordained that you should.

Again, Paul can lend some insight here. As he tells us in his letter to the church at Ephesus, "God saved you by his grace when you believed. And you can't take credit for this; it is a gift from God. Salvation is not a reward for the good things we have done, so none of us can boast about it. For we are God's masterpiece. He has created us anew in Christ Jesus, so we can do the good things he planned for us long ago" (Eph. 2:8–10). In the same way, when God wants to do something significant in our churches, it is because of his grace, not our own merit. Who are we to keep him from exercising that right by refusing to think big and failing to invite him to do more than we are capable of dreaming? We are his handiwork, created to do the good things he planned for us—not simply the things that we think make sense in our understanding of the typical weekend service routine.

Your big day is a good work that God prepared in advance. Just as he showed himself on the day of Pentecost, he wants to show himself in your church, and mine, in surprising ways. All we have to do is seek him, allow him to set the goals, cover everything in prayer, and then play the role assigned to us. That's where our part of the process, and the actual evangelism system, begins to ramp up. We have the task of preparing for the harvest.

The Harvest

The evangelism system we'll be discussing in the following pages will give you the tools you need to prepare for, and keep the fruit from, your big day. Think of the big day as a tool in your evangelism toolbox. It is an incredible way to reach lots of people at one time and immensely effective in taking your church to the next level. But if you don't prepare for and follow up on the big day correctly, God won't show his full power through it and you won't be able to sustain your momentum after the day ends. That's where the evangelism system kicks in.

The evangelism system begins when an unchurched person is prompted by the Spirit to attend your church and ends when that person follows Jesus Christ, is baptized publicly, and is moving toward membership. By deciding to do a big day, scheduling the day wisely, covering the day in prayer, and setting an attendance goal, you are paving the way for the large numbers of first-time guests God wants to bring to your church. But there's still a lot of work to be done. Your big day has to be couched in a system that can help you prepare for and then support the momentum it is going to bring. If you do a big day without the underlying system in place, you may have one great Sunday, but things will quickly fall back to the status quo.

As I mentioned in the introduction, at The Journey we believe that "to evangelize is to invite others through the power of the Holy Spirit to put their trust in God through Jesus Christ, to accept Jesus as their Savior and follow Him as their leader in everyday life as members of a local church." To be able to truly evangelize, we have to do our part to prepare for those people God wants to prompt

> *The evangelism system begins when an unchurched person is prompted by the Spirit to attend your church and ends when that person follows Jesus Christ, is baptized publicly, and is moving toward membership.*

our way and put the work in to harvest the fruit once they have stepped through our doors. Your big day is an important piece of a much larger puzzle.

Let's define the broad parameters of the evangelism system. The system is made up of four parts, which organize the rest of this book's contents:

1. **Pastor:** Evangelism begins with the pastor. He is the one who guides the strategy and establishes the church's culture.
2. **Personal evangelism:** Personal evangelism is how your church shares its faith on a personal level. How open are people to inviting their friends to church? Are they living

out their faith in such a way that they are influencing people toward Jesus? Is there a high level of relational evangelism going on in your community?

3. **Promotion:** Promotion is the key element in letting your community know that your church exists. How do you sow seeds of the gospel into the community? Promotion can also be thought of as your marketing plan.

4. **Preservation:** Evangelism does little good if you aren't able to preserve the fruit that God gives you. How do you make sure everyone who shows up for your big day comes back the next week? How do you know and acknowledge when someone accepts Christ? Then how do you encourage him to keep growing in his faith?

Evangelism doesn't happen in a vacuum. God has to be at work in an unchurched person's life, making her ready to step out on faith. She has to know that your church exists and looks inviting. She has to receive an invitation and know what to do with it. A system has to be in place that makes her feel welcome when she decides to walk through your doors. You have to follow up with her properly after her visit so that she doesn't fall through the cracks. All of these factors weave into and support the definition of evangelism that I've put forth. And the four corners of the evangelism system—pastor, personal evangelism, promotion, and preservation—create the framework through which God will show his power. As you know, God doesn't usually work in a vacuum either. He prefers to use his creation, you and me, as his hands and feet. We just have to qualify by being willing to put in the work we are called to. When we do, God will give us the distinct honor of using our churches to bring people into his kingdom.

pastor

4

reaching the boiling point

*Taking Your Evangelistic Temp
and Turning Up the Heat*

But since you are like lukewarm water, neither hot nor cold, I
will spit you out of my mouth!

Revelation 3:16

We cannot become what we need to be by remaining what we
are.

Max Depree

During the Vietnam War, Admiral James Stockdale was the highest-ranking U.S. officer taken as a prisoner by the Vietnamese. During the eight years that Stockdale was held hostage, he was tortured regularly. He had no reason to think he would ever be released or see his family again. Yet, despite his horrific circumstances, Stockdale became a beacon of hope for the other prisoners in the camp. He developed secret modes of communication to keep away the inevitable effects of isolation. He taught the other prisoners how to create coping mechanisms to deal with the enemy's torture tactics. In short, he kept faith alive in a situation where most people would have long since let it die.

Jim Collins, author of *Good to Great*, had the opportunity to spend some time with Stockdale on the Stanford University campus they share. Reflecting on their conversations, Collins writes, "What separates people, Stockdale taught me, is not the presence or absence of difficulty, but how they deal with the inevitable difficulties of life. In wrestling with challenges, the Stockdale Paradox has proven powerful for coming back from difficulties not weakened, but stronger."[1]

What has become known as the Stockdale Paradox states that in every circumstance, you must retain faith that you will prevail in the end regardless of the difficulties *and at the same time* confront the most brutal facts of your current reality, whatever they might be. During his eight years as a POW, Stockdale looked the reality of his situation squarely in the face each day, yet he never lost faith that he would eventually prevail. And he did. After the war, Stockdale became the first three-star officer in the navy's history to earn both aviator wings and the Congressional Medal of Honor.

Now, you and I are church leaders. We are not in prison camps facing daily torture. Yet we can learn a great deal from the Stockdale Paradox. First of all, while we are not fighting with guns and tanks, we are engaged in a spiritual war each and every day. We have an enemy who wants to keep us and our churches ineffective. That enemy hates evangelism. Second, we know what we want the end of our story to look like. For us, prevailing in evangelism means that we do our part to bring as many unchurched people to God as possible—as many as he would have us bring. That's an intimidating thought when you again consider Matthew 28:19: "Therefore, go and make disciples of all the nations, baptizing them in the name of the Father and the Son and the Holy Spirit." Third, in order to prevail we have to be honest about our current reality.

Checking the Temperature

Think of your current level of evangelism as a reading on a thermometer. What is the evangelistic temperature in your church? Are you boiling hot or freezing cold? Or are you somewhere in the middle? Regardless of where you are at the moment, you have to take the Stockdale Paradox to heart. It's time to confront the most brutal facts of your current reality while at the same time retaining faith that you will prevail in the end. No matter what the evangelistic temperature of your church is today, you can take steps to raise the temperature until it is boiling over. How? Everything begins with the pastor.

When it comes to evangelism, the pastor's primary role is to keep the evangelistic temperature red-hot inside the church. Organizations of any kind, churches included, tend to become inwardly focused if no one has committed to keeping them outwardly focused. An inward turning is natural and inevitable as a church's self-interests work themselves to the forefront—which they will do. We get busy taking care of our staff, ministering to those in our congregation, meeting the budget, preparing for the weekend, and before we know it, we've forgotten all about the salvation of John and Joan in the coffee shop down the street. It becomes all about us, to the detriment of our evangelistic intentions.

The only hope we ever have of raising the evangelistic temperature in the church is to make sure that the church's leader—the pastor—takes on his proper leadership role and keeps the church focused on reaching others for Jesus. If you are the pastor, it doesn't matter whether you are a gifted evangelist or not. You may have someone else in your church who loves evangelism so much that you are tempted to turn over the reins on this issue. Don't do it. You must lead. The church will head in the direction you lead them. You have to put in the work to keep your church members and attenders looking outside themselves.

But first, you need to take your church's temperature. Measure and face the reality of your current evangelistic state. Think of a thermometer whose scale is 0 to 100. That means 0 is frozen and 100 is boiling over, on fire, ignited, the absolute peak of evangelistic effectiveness. Where does your church fall? What's the temperature? To get a gauge, take a hard look at these six areas of your church and try ranking each one individually from 0 to 100:

- **How many people are accepting Jesus as their Savior?** How do you know when someone commits their life to Christ? Are you keeping track of and evaluating the numbers? Temperature: _____
- **How many baptisms are you doing?** I believe that baptism is the best New Testament measurement for evangelism, as I discuss below. How often do you baptize new believers?

54

(For a free resource on how to overcome the barriers to baptism, visit www.ignitebook.com.)

Temperature: _____

- **How many of your people are bringing their friends to church?** At The Journey, we have found that 87 percent of our first-time guests come because a friend invited them. Using a Connection Card in our service (see *Fusion: Turning First-Time Guests into Fully-Engaged Members of Your Church*) helps us gauge this. As people are filling out their cards, we simply say, "If you are here for the first time today and a friend invited you, just write that friend's name somewhere on your Connection Card, so we know." And they do.

Temperature: _____

- **How many first-time guests do you have?** First-time guests are not necessarily unchurched, but this is still a good measurement. Five first-time guests per one hundred attenders is a good ratio to average.

Temperature: _____

- **How many evangelistic outreaches do you have scheduled?** Your evangelistic outreaches should be scheduled on your calendar well in advance so you can mobilize people to participate. Pastor, if you aren't showing up for these outreaches—especially early on in your church's evangelism efforts—you can't expect anyone else to show up either.

Temperature: _____

- **How often are you praying for the unchurched?** Are the unchurched part of your general culture of prayer? Do you encourage your growth group leaders to pray for their unchurched friends and to encourage their group members to do the same? Again, as you steer people to pray for the unchurched, their hearts will be steered toward the unchurched.

Temperature: _____

How did you do? What is your average temperature reading? Are you operating as the frozen chosen or are you close to the boiling point? If you feel like your evangelistic temperature is on the cold side, that's okay—right now. The fact that you are reading this book shows that you have a heart to reach more people. Courageously face your current reality.

Raised to Walk

While these six points of measurement taken together will help you gauge the evangelistic temperature of your church, one point stands alone better than the others. Baptisms can be a fair and consistent signal of whether or not evangelism is happening as you go forward. So consider again the question "How many baptisms are you doing?" Baptism is both a metaphor and a symbol for what Christianity is all about. As Paul explains it, when a person walks into the water, they represent their life before Christ. Their immersion represents the washing away of their sins through Jesus's sacrifice on the cross. And when they are raised out of the water, they are being raised into a fresh life, ready to go forth as a new creation in Jesus. (For more on baptism, see appendix 1, "Baptism.")

As I've mentioned, the evangelism system is a success when a person who walked through your doors unchurched makes their profession of faith public through baptism. That's the exciting payoff! God has used you and your church to make himself real in that person's life. Ensure that baptism is the joyful occasion it deserves to be. Have people invite their friends and family. Baptism is not just a religious tradition; it's a celebration of brand-new life. And it is your signal that true evangelism is happening. You know that God is working when you see new people telling the world about their young faith by following Jesus in baptism. Down the road, once your evangelism system is in place and running well, let me encourage you to keep a constant eye on your baptisms as the ongoing gauge of your evangelistic temperature.

It's Getting Hot in Here

Peter Drucker once said, "Efficiency is doing things right; effectiveness is doing the right things." Every pastor needs to be doing three right things to raise the temperature of evangelism. I'll spend the rest of this section detailing those three things. If you are a senior pastor, understand that your role in this system is crucial, as you are about to see. I say to you now, as Paul said to Timothy, "You should keep a clear mind in every situation. Don't be afraid of suffering for the Lord. Work at telling others the Good News, and fully carry out the ministry God has given you" (2 Tim. 4:5).

The work of evangelism is not easy. Never forget the enemy who wants, with everything in his power, to resist your efforts. There will be suffering, just as Paul said. Complacent Christians will likely leave your church when you raise the evangelistic temperature. You may work for a season without seeing your desired results. But the harvest will come if you continue to sow the seed. This principle cannot be changed. As you move forward and begin to put the evangelism system together, remember: always face your current reality, no matter how bad it seems, *and* keep faith in the ultimate plan and purpose that God has for your church.

Church Leader Testimony

Since we started implementing the evangelism system, we have seen our average weekly attendance increase 10 to 20 percent. The system also helped our church break our most recent growth barrier. We are now planning on adding a second service and looking to expand our facilities. God has truly used the evangelism system in our church to reach more people.

Trent Carpenter, Lead Pastor
Cross Community Church (South Point, OH)

5

setting the stage

Successfully Leveraging Your Influence

Care for the flock that God has entrusted to you. Watch over it willingly, not grudgingly—not for what you will get out of it, but because you are eager to serve God.

1 Peter 5:2

A teacher affects eternity; he can never tell where his influence stops.

Henry Brooks Adams

As the lights come up in the auditorium, Pastor Tim steps to the center of the stage once again. "What a great day we've had here at FCC! I'm so glad you all have been a part of it. If you found today's message helpful, why not invite a friend or co-worker to join you next week? We'll be talking about how to handle money in a way that pleases God. So if you know anyone who is under financial strain, I especially encourage you to invite them to come with you. Have a great week! We'll see you next Sunday."

Tim heads backstage for a little quiet time before the next service. On the way to his study, he runs into Sam. Sam has been a leader in the church for over three years. He serves almost every Sunday in one capacity or another. Tim always sees him welcoming guests, manning the refreshments table, or ushering people to their seats. Today Sam is working backstage to make sure the service runs smoothly.

"Hey, Pastor Tim!"

"Hi, Sam. How are you today?"

"I'm great. Even better now. Good message."

"Thanks!" Tim throws up his hand in farewell and starts to walk away.

"Hey, Pastor," Sam says quickly. "Do you have a second? I've got a question for you."

"Sure. What's up?" Tim steps back over.

"There's this guy at my office. His name is Jon. For some reason, I really feel like God wants me to get him here to FCC. The thing is, I've asked him to come to church with me three or four times and he keeps turning me down. It's getting a little embarrassing."

"I'm proud of you for asking him more than once, Sam. That's good. Lots of people stop asking if they get rejected just once, but it often takes several invitations before someone will say yes to checking out a church. God has to be working in their lives. By continuing to ask, you are leaving that door open."

"So should I ask again right away, or let it lie for a little while?"

"You know what? Why don't you wait a couple of weeks." Tim steps a little farther into the corner and motions for Sam to join him. "I haven't made this announcement to the church yet, but in about a month and a half, we are going to be having a really big day around here. I'm going to kick off a new teaching series, and we're going to put out a challenge to everyone to invite their friends and co-workers. It'll be a chance for us to impact the community in a big way."

"Nice!"

"So," Tim continues, "wait two or three weeks. Keep building your friendship with Jon. And then, when we start promoting the big day, I'll give you some tools that will make the invitation a little easier and may even motivate him to say yes this time."

"That sounds great, Pastor. That's what I'll do. . . . Huh. I can't wait to hear more about this big day!"

"The guy at your office—Jon. Is he married?" asks Tim.

"Yep. His wife's name is Liz," says Sam.

"Jon and Liz. I'll be praying for them." At that, Pastor Tim puts a hand on Sam's shoulder and says, "Thanks for serving, Sam. Things run a lot better around here because of you."

"Anytime, Pastor! And hey, thanks for the 'tip.'"

Those of us who are pastors have been given a unique opportunity, one that too often we take for granted. Each and every time you step in front of your crowd, you have the chance to influence them for Jesus. You have the opportunity to speak truth into their lives—truth that God wants them to hear. Whether

61

you are preaching from a stage to thousands of listeners, from a pulpit to hundreds, or from a makeshift sanctuary to just a handful, you have been given incredible power to shape the lives and eternities of every person listening to you. That's exactly why the responsibility for keeping the evangelistic temperature in the church at the boiling point falls on you.

> *The pastor's strategic use of sermons, challenges, announcements, and vision casting from the stage (pulpit) can raise the evangelistic temperature of the church.*

A pastor can raise the level of evangelism in his church in three ways. They are (1) through the *stage*, (2) through the *staff*, and (3) through the church's *structure*. We'll deal with staff and structure in the next chapter. For now, I want you to wrap your mind fully around the position God has given you on the stage, if you are a lead pastor. If you are not a lead pastor, you still need to understand the significance of this position. Church leaders of any kind must be able to support their lead pastor in his attempts to use the stage for optimal effectiveness.

We tend to underestimate the influence the pastor has to motivate people, challenge people, and encourage people to live an evangelistic lifestyle. There are points in every service that you can take advantage of to raise the value of what's important. Your strategic use of sermons, challenges, announcements, and vision casting from the stage can raise the evangelistic temperature of the church quicker than anything else.

I've noticed that what gets presented from the stage is more likely to get accomplished in the pews. In other words, you can't keep quiet and assume that your people will do anything. You can't hope that something is going to happen. Hope is not a strategy. You have to challenge. You have to encourage. You even have to push a little. The Bible tells us repeatedly that as pastors, we have the responsibility of shepherding the flock that is under our care. Shepherds don't just hope that their flocks will head in the right direction; they actively lead their flocks in the right direction. As should we.

Note how Pastor Tim used his last few minutes of the service at FCC to encourage his people to bring a friend to church with them next week. We issue the same challenge at The Journey every single Sunday. After every service we say, "If you found today's message helpful, why not invite a friend to join you next week?" If I know that the next week's topic is going to be aimed at a widespread felt need, I'll mention that. "Next week we are going to be talking about dealing with stress in marriage. If you know someone who might find that message helpful, bring them with you." Consistently challenging people to reach out to their friends and invite people to church is one of the ways you can use the stage to add heat to your evangelistic thermometer. Following are five more.

Tell Your Own Evangelistic Stories

The best way you can create a heart for evangelism with your people is by sharing your personal evangelism stories. There's power in being able to say, "You know, last week when I was sharing my faith with someone . . ." or "Yesterday when I invited my neighbor to church. . . ." As soon as you begin telling a story from your own life, it's like you've just picked up a megaphone.

Your people tune in. They connect with what you are saying. But you have to have these stories to tell. If you aren't reaching out to the unchurched, you can't talk about reaching out to the unchurched with integrity.

As a pastor, I know it is much easier to teach on evangelism than it is to live an evangelistic lifestyle. A few Easters ago, I decided that the people on my staff should hold each other accountable for inviting their unchurched friends to the Easter service. I was really excited about this challenge until it hit me that I couldn't even begin to issue it until I knew who I was going to invite. Now, I usually keep a list of the unchurched people I know so that I can pray for them and reach out. But several people on my list had moved away. I found myself in an uncomfortable position—I was going to have to find some new unchurched people to invite to the Easter service. Here I was, the pastor of a church whose ultimate mission was to bring people to Jesus, and I didn't know any unbelievers. How could I challenge my people to invite their lost friends when I didn't even have any lost friends? I couldn't. I had to start prayerfully building that list back up by stepping outside of the bubble.

We all slip into the trap of being so busy in our Christian circles that we lose touch with the unbelieving world. But we will never be able to relate to or impact unbelievers if we don't take the time to reach out and develop relationships with them. We need to be mindful to follow Jesus's example in this area. Consider Mark 2:16–17:

> But when the teachers of religious law who were Pharisees saw him eating with tax collectors and other sinners, they asked his disciples, "Why does he eat with such scum?" When Jesus heard this, he told them, "Healthy people don't need a doctor—sick

people do. I have come to call not those who think they are righteous, but those who know they are sinners."

Take a moment to think about your own life. How many relationships do you have with people who don't know Jesus? In fact, let me encourage you to write down the names of at least five unchurched people you are currently, personally influencing toward Jesus:

1. _____
2. _____
3. _____
4. _____
5. _____
6. _____
7. _____
8. _____
9. _____
10. _____

Could you write five names? I gave you ten blanks to encourage you to pray for ten people that you can reach out to for Jesus. Make sure you haven't become so consumed with doing church that you have left the work of bringing in the unsaved to the people in your congregation. They will not do what you do not model. Part of shepherding the flock is personally going out and finding the stray sheep.

Testimonies

Speaking of megaphones, people also tune in to stories of life change—especially when they recognize some aspect of themselves in those stories. That's why personal testimonies are so effective. Having members of your congregation share testimonies from the stage is a great way to promote evangelism in your church. Testimonies are among your most powerful tools for motivating your people.

You can incorporate testimonies into your service in several ways. You can have someone speak from the stage just before the message. You can bring the testimony in halfway through the message, especially if it illustrates a point you've been teaching. We've also done testimonies via video on the big screens. The power is in the story itself. You are presenting a changed life to everyone in the crowd. When done well, a testimony will raise people's excitement over what God can do and encourage them to ask themselves, "Why would I keep God's goodness a secret? He changes lives!" Up goes the temperature.

Let me give a word of caution here: make sure that you are strategic in your use of testimonies. If you are preaching a message on small groups, ask one of your most relatable small group leaders to give a testimony that Sunday. Ask her weeks in advance so that she can come prepared. You may even want to have her write out her story and share it with you or a staff pastor first. The testimonies you incorporate are meant to serve a specific purpose. If you are in a smaller church, don't be tempted to open the pulpit to anyone who feels like sharing. That will create confusion and probably scare any unbelievers in your crowd to death. It sure won't raise the evangelistic temperature of your church. I'm not saying that you should never create an environment where people can share. Small groups are great for that. But on Sunday mornings, keep things simple.

Teach an Evangelism Series

Ever been asked, "What's your five-year plan?" Lots of people
have a five- or even ten-year plan. I have a three-year plan—for
sermon series rotation, that is. Every three years, I teach an entire
sermon series on evangelism, in an effort to keep our evangelistic
temperature high. Every three years, I also teach an entire series
on stewardship and one on ministry or volunteerism. The plan
plays out like this: Year one, I teach on evangelism. Year two, I
teach on ministry. Year three, I teach on stewardship. Year four,
back to evangelism. You get the picture. I can't teach an entire
series on evangelism, one on stewardship, and one on ministry
every year. But this three-year plan ensures that at least once
every three years, my congregation gets a four- to five-week
series on the ins and outs of evangelism.

Don't misunderstand—you should teach messages that point
your people toward evangelism several times every year. And you
should be reminding them about evangelism continually, in the
various ways we are discussing. But every three years, you can
do a full-fledged study of the biblical basis of evangelism, how
and why to witness, how to get over the fear of sharing your
faith, ways to reach out to the community, living the example
. . . and the possibilities go on. (For samples of sermon series
we've done, visit www.ignitebook.com.)

If things are going well in your church, you will inevitably have
some first-time guests in the house for many of your evangelism
messages, both when you do a series and for single messages
throughout the year. Make sure that you address them before you
launch into your evangelism discussion. I like to say something
along these lines: "Today I am going to be talking to those people
who call The Journey home. I'm talking to the Christians in our

audience, because one of the things we have to do as Christians is to be quick to share our faith with those who are not yet Christians. If you are here today and you aren't yet a Christian, you actually picked a great day to come. You are going to get a behind-the-scenes look at what Christianity is all about."

I have found that we have as many people, if not more, give their life to Christ after a "how-to" evangelism message as we do after a message on an everyday issue from the Bible. Why? Because those unbelievers get a sense of the passion we have about evangelism. They realize we are really behind the faith we profess and have a heart to share its truth with them. They want to be a part of what's going on. Just as the early church was known for its zeal, so should we be. We need to share our enthusiasm and never neglect to call those listening to make a commitment to Jesus.

Give Immediate Opportunities for Action

If you have just preached a message on evangelism, make sure you give your people an immediate opportunity to live out what they've just learned. Say it's Palm Sunday and you have just preached a passionate message about the importance of inviting people to church for Easter Sunday. Back that up by giving them a way to act. Have invitation cards printed before the service and give each person four or five cards as they leave. They can use those cards as a tool to invite people to the Easter service. You are making it easier for them to take immediate action.

Around The Journey, we love the idea of servant evangelism. If you aren't familiar with servant evangelism, it's the concept of showing God's love by meeting a practical need while at the same time inviting someone to church. For example, a great servant evangelism project is to stand on a busy downtown street corner and hand each passerby a free pack of gum and a postcard invitation to your church. Often, when I am teaching on evangelism, I will make sure that our people take it to heart by challenging them to do a servant evangelism outreach right after the service.

One Sunday I preached a message about loving the people of our city. You know, encouraging the congregation to appreciate the community we've been placed in and to reach out to its members at every opportunity. While I was teaching, I had a team of volunteers go out and buy three hundred dozen hot Krispy Kreme doughnuts and set the boxes up on tables in the lobby. I was busy asking everyone in the service, "How many of you believe we should love our city?" They all raised their hands. "How many of you think we should start reaching out immediately?" Again, all hands in the air. Then I said, "Great. Here's what we are going to do. On your way out, I'm going to give you a box of Krispy Kremes and some information about our church. Go find someone working in the city—a police officer, a doorman, someone in an office—deliver these donuts and the invitation, and tell them that you are just doing it to show God's love in a practical way." There were a lot of happy firemen in New York City that day. And a lot of believers who got a little more comfortable reaching out for God. We'll talk more about servant evangelism in chapter 8.

Utilize a Preaching Calendar

Our lives are full of natural cycles. God set things up that way. As church leaders, we need to be aware of the flow God has put in place and go with it. One of the best ways to take advantage of that flow is to manage your preaching calendar. You can plan in advance to maximize the natural evangelistic times of the year. As I mentioned previously, at certain times of the year unbelievers are more likely to be open to the message of the gospel than others. In order to make sure you preach messages that connect with the unchurched during those times, you need to know what you are going to preach several months, or ideally a year, in advance. If you don't, you will miss vital opportunities for evangelism.

Planning your big days is a huge part of utilizing a preaching calendar correctly. As we discussed in chapter 2, you will be most likely to get the largest number of new people to your church in February, at Easter, and one month after school begins. So those three big day opportunities should be the cornerstones of your calendar. You preach a big attraction series in February and kick it off with a big day. Then you let things settle in March while you assimilate the new people that February's big day brought you. You build the momentum for Easter Sunday over the weeks preceding that big day. Easter comes. You kick off a new four- to six-week sermon series and encourage all of your guests to keep coming back for its duration. You grow.

I coached a pastor in Florida whose church's attendance had been flat for several years. We decided to see what putting a real spotlight on evangelism at the right time of year could do in his church. We didn't have time to plan a full-fledged big day for Easter, so I just encouraged him to use Palm Sunday to preach on evangelism. At the end of the service, he asked everyone to write down the names of three to ten people they knew who didn't attend church. Then he prayed over those names and issued a special challenge to everyone to bring those friends to the Easter service. He went from an average of 700 people to 1,400 on Easter. Of course, not all 1,400 came back the next Sunday—but 900 did. By taking a couple of simple steps to raise the evangelistic temperature in his church, he grew his church by 200 people. He started assimilating them and planning for the next true big day opportunity.

Remember to schedule your fall big day for one month after school begins. The momentum from the fall will take you to Christmas, where you have another natural surge you can take advantage of. Then all eyes turn back to February. Many of you may have noticed that you automatically have more first-time guests in September and February, but you never knew why. Now that you understand the natural rhythms of the year and how to plan big days to take advantage of them, you can begin to maximize and keep that growth. (For a free copy of my best-selling resource "Planning a One Year Preaching Calendar," visit www.ignitebook.com.)

Preaching Calendar Example

Time	Evangelistic Purpose	Result
January	Build excitement for February	People invite 3 friends
February	Kick off high attraction series	Break attendance record
Palm Sunday	Challenge people to invite 3–10 friends	People invite 3–10 friends
Easter	Start new series; challenge new people to stay	Break attendance record
August	Build excitement for fall series	People invite 3 friends
September/October	Kick off new series	Break attendance record
December	Promote Christmas services to community	Reach new people

Not many would argue the leadership ability of the late president Dwight Eisenhower, who once said from his stage,

"Leadership is the art of getting someone else to do something you want done because he wants to do it." You have the unique opportunity to get people to do what God wants done because they want to do it. That's a power not to be taken lightly. Use it wisely and always keep the evangelistic temperature of your church boiling hot. What you do from the stage each Sunday affects eternity. You have no idea where its influence stops.

6

carrying the torch

Igniting Your Church's Structure

But be sure that everything is done properly and in order.

1 Corinthians 14:40

The people's capacity to achieve is determined by their leader's ability to empower.

John Maxwell

One of the greatest parenting lessons I've learned is that children usually live up—or down—to your expectations. For example, if your child doing well in school is an inherent, unquestioned expectation around your house, he probably will. If you expect your daughter to keep her room clean from an early age, she'll usually live up to that. Children are good at reading the emotional climate and intrinsic expectations around them from an early age, and acting accordingly. Recently, I was in a crowded restaurant and overheard one parent say to the other, in earshot of their seemingly content five-year-old, "He's exhausted. I'll be amazed if we make it out of here without a tantrum." Guess what happened about three minutes later? Their expectations were met.

This truth goes for adults too. Ever notice how the co-worker you expect shoddy work from continues to come through? Some would argue that in adults expectations follow evidence. You expect shoddy work from that co-worker because that's what he's given you since the day he started the job. But I believe that if you make a point of expecting more from him—of holding him to a higher standard—his level of work will improve. As Goethe wisely said so long ago, "If we treat people as they are, we make them worse. If we treat people as they ought to be, we help them become what they are capable of becoming." You have to empower people by expecting the absolute best from them while consistently challenging them to give you that best. In fact, that's one of the keys to keeping the evangelistic temperature of your church hot.

How Hot Is Your Staff . . . for Evangelism?

In the last chapter, we discussed the pastor's responsibility in using the stage to keep the evangelistic temperature at the boiling point. The second way a pastor can keep things toasty is to challenge his staff to hold the torch close to the thermostat. If you, as the pastor, are going to lead on this issue, you have to expect a high level of evangelistic involvement from your staff, and you have to hold them accountable to those expectations. I would go so far as to encourage you to make a heart for evangelism one of the standard prerequisites for all new hires.

I want you to latch on to two key words beneath this canopy of expectation: *challenge* and *accountable*. When it comes to raising the evangelistic temperature through your staff, you have to challenge them to be actively involved in evangelism, and then you have to hold them accountable for what you've asked them to do. If you challenge and hold your staff accountable in the following four areas, you will see their passion for evangelism ignite and the reading on the thermometer climb:

1. **Serve in evangelistic activities**—Put servant evangelism and other outreaches on your calendar weeks in advance so that your staff and key leaders can plan to be there. Let them know that being a leader in your church means going out and serving. They can't slide under the radar.
2. **Pray for unchurched friends**—Challenge your staff and key lay leaders to pray regularly for their unchurched friends. You can hold them accountable by setting up an accountability partner system.
3. **Pray and fast for big days**—Encourage your staff and other leaders to participate in a time of fasting and prayer before your big days. Just imagine what it would look like if, before your next big day, as you are challenging the church to invite their friends, your staff and key leaders are praying and fasting for the day. Think about the resulting infusion of spiritual power. (For an overview of fasting, see appendix 2. For a free resource on fasting, visit www.ignitebook.com.)

Before big days at The Journey, we usually put this challenge out to anyone in the church who wants to participate. Of course, not everyone who says they are going to join in the fasting and prayer will actually do it, but their hearts and minds will be more attuned to the big day simply because they considered the commitment. Your staff, on the other hand, should be required to fast and pray— and, again, to hold each other accountable. Whenever I involve our staff in a time of fasting and prayer, I make sure to take the opportunity to point our focus outward. I remind people to pray for those in need throughout our community. The evangelistic temperature in our church always rises as a result.

4. **Invite friends to church**—From time to time, I will ask people on my staff, "Who have you invited to church lately?" or "Who was the last unchurched friend to come to church with you?" They know to expect the question at random, which keeps them accountable for reaching out to their friends. They understand that they aren't going to stay on staff at The Journey for very long if they aren't inviting people to church. It's simply part of the culture. It's the standard. We talk about this inherent expectation in staff meetings. The challenge is continually out there, and I do all I can to keep them on their toes.

For one recent big day, I asked my staff to write the names of the unchurched friends they were planning to invite on the whiteboard in our main conference area. If they could only write one name, their first challenge was to go out and build some intentional relationships with unchurched people (like I had to do for the Easter service I mentioned!). Every day, they had to walk in and see those names staring at them on the whiteboard—names of people who needed Jesus; names of people they were taking responsibility for.

That challenge gave many of them the little extra push they needed to step beyond their comfort zones and make the invitation. Remember: if someone isn't sharing his faith, he's not growing in his faith. Do you really want people on your staff who aren't growing in their faith? Raise the bar and you'll be amazed how many will climb over it with you.

Stoking through Structure

The third and final way a pastor can raise the evangelistic temperature in his church is through the church's structure. Too often, pastors create an atmosphere within their churches that impedes evangelism. They try to exert too much control. They focus their attention on inner workings instead of on the vision for reaching the community. They downplay evangelism because they have a high level of peace and comfort with the status quo. God doesn't do grand acts of evangelism in churches that aren't structured to receive them.

Rick Warren has often said, "You have to decide whether to structure for growth or control. You cannot have both." Take a minute to think about the underlying structure of your church, as it relates to evangelism. Have you structured for growth? Have you structured with an eye to the greater community? Have you structured in a way that helps you mobilize your people for evangelism? We've already looked at the importance of building big days into your structure. Let's look at four other ways you can make sure you are continually raising the temperature through your structure:

1. **Plan regular evangelistic events**—These are the outreach events that you will be challenging your staff and key leaders to participate in, as we discussed above. Make sure that your evangelistic events aren't makeshift. Plan them well in advance. Start putting the word out immediately. If you haven't been doing many outreach events, don't let the idea intimidate you. Just make a decision to get started. Do something. Plan an event or two and put them on the calendar.

   Summertime is one of the best times of the year for evangelistic outreach. Not only are people out and about, and therefore easier to connect with, but there's also a principle working in your favor: if you plant seed in the summer, you'll reap the harvest in the fall. To put it another way, you can either plant in the summer or beg in the fall. The choice is up to you. So plan a car wash. Pass out bottles of water and postcard invitations in your local park. Prayer walk through a new neighborhood. Plan some events so you can get people involved in evangelism. What you do over the summer will feed right into your fall big day. (For a free report on "How to Maximize Summer," visit www. ignitebook.com.)

2. **Structure for celebration**—Build opportunities for consistently celebrating evangelism into your church's structure. We use a lot of media at The Journey. We always videotape our baptism celebrations, complete with brief testimonies from the people who are being baptized, and

then edit the footage into a two- or three-minute piece to be shown in a weekend service. We want everyone to see the celebration of life change that is happening as a result of our willingness to reach out. (To view a recent baptism video from The Journey, visit www.ignitebook.com.)

Inevitably, several of the people being baptized always say something along the lines of, "I hadn't been in church for years, and then my friend from school invited me to come with him," or "I was just walking down the street one day and this girl handed me a pack of gum and an invitation to her church. It was at just the right time because I had really been seeking. . . ." When the congregation hears these stories, they get excited about the evidence of changed lives. That in turn gives them a renewed sense of the power of evangelism. And up goes the temperature.

3. **Engage small groups in evangelism**—From time to time, encourage your small groups to do a "mini" study on evangelism as a part of their regular semester—either as a break from the regular, weekly curriculum or after they've finished it. Have them read a book on sharing their faith and lead them to hold each other accountable for doing so. Taking two or three weeks to underscore the importance of evangelism and to give your small group members some tools for reaching out is well worth the effort and planning.

4. **Allow people to belong before they believe**—There are three stages to faith for many people: (1) believing, (2) belonging, and (3) becoming. Most churches operate as if these stages happen in sequential order. They think that

to be a part of the church, you have to first believe. Then you can belong. And over time, you'll truly become.

In reality, these stages are much more fluid. They can happen in any order. Often stage 2 or stage 3 precedes stage 1. In other words, sometimes people need to belong before they can believe. Many people come to your church looking for something other than God. Maybe they want to make some new connections. Maybe they want to be involved in something bigger than themselves but haven't yet come to a place of belief. Let them belong first. Let them become. What's wrong with allowing an unbeliever to serve at the refreshments table if it will get him to church and let him interact with some Christians? What's wrong with letting him usher someone to a seat? Sometimes unbelievers need this association with the Christian world in order to figure out what faith is all about. They need to rub shoulders with believers.

Now, I'm not suggesting that you allow an unbeliever to lead worship or count your offering. You will need to set commonsense guidelines for your environment. But we need to stop putting up unintentional barriers through our structure. If we let people move a little further into our circles before they believe, they will get to know us and have a stronger desire to grasp on to the source of peace and joy they see in us.

God will never give you more than you are prepared to handle. He won't work through your church unless you are willing to work with him. By making sure that you, as the pastor, are doing your part to keep the evangelistic temperature of your church at the boiling point, you are saying to God, "Yes, I am ready and willing to hold up my end of this deal. I will keep the church passionate for evangelism so that you might work through us to draw people into your kingdom." As you use the stage wisely, expect the best of your staff, and structure your church for evangelism, you will be cooperating with God in reaching people for his glory. May you be amazed at how he uses you to bolster the waves of evangelism he wants to pour through your church.

personal evangelism

7

mobilizing for evangelism

Releasing the Army

The first thing Andrew did was to find his brother, Simon, and tell him, "We have found the Messiah" (that is, the Christ). And he brought him to Jesus.

John 1:41–42 NIV

Instilling urgency . . . is critical to getting organizations to switch directions; arguing the . . . case using facts alone won't create that urgency.

John P. Kotter

Relationships are powerful tools that carry tremendous influence. When we have even a vague connection with another person, that connection plays into our decision making and our actions. We buy from salespeople we like. We recommend acquaintances for the new position we've just heard about. We meet our wife's old roommate's cousin for dinner when he's in town. Why? Well, because he's our wife's old roommate's cousin and doesn't know anyone else in the area. Okay, maybe that's just me. But it's true that in a world of seven billion people, we latch on to the connections around us. We harness the power of the old "who you know" and we put it to work.

> *Sixty to 80 percent of first-time guests come to church because a friend invited them.*

The closer those relationships, the more influence they have in our daily lives. I bet you would do just about anything your mother asked you to do, whether you wanted to or not. She's your mother. In the same way, most of us take requests from our friends seriously. If a friend invites you to take part in an activity or event, you will generally say yes right away, based on your level of interest and the strength of that relationship. If your best friend asks you to go to his son's Little League games, you'll eventually go—even if you are allergic to kids and not a fan of baseball. You do it because he's your friend and he wants you there. That's reason enough. If, on the other hand, you've been hoping to catch a Little League game soon anyway, then all the better. You'll probably go the first time he asks.

In the church world, we often fail to recognize the influence of the friend relationship. We have a vague sense of "Oh, I wish my people would invite their friends to church," but we don't tap into the true potential of that idea. At The Journey and in churches I have coached, I've found that 60 to 80 percent of first-time guests in a growing church come because a friend invited them. Sixty to 80 percent! Wouldn't you say that's a percentage worth cultivating? But don't just take it from me. In his article "Evangelism: The Why and How," church growth expert Elmer Towns reports an even higher percentage. He asserts that 86 percent of new converts say they came to church for the first time because of an invitation from a friend or relative.[1] I have also discovered that about one in four people will attend church with a friend the first time they are invited. Multiple invitations eventually yield visits from at least three out of four of those friends. When you think about these stats in relation to the number of regular attenders and members in your church, you should get excited.

This leads me back to the question I mentioned in the introduction. That is, we should be able to ask ourselves, "Why *don't* we double every week?" Are you ready for the answer? As church leaders, we aren't mobilizing our people for evangelism. We haven't been equipping them for the mission. Paul clearly tells us in Ephesians 4:11–12, "Now these are the gifts Christ gave to the church: the apostles, the prophets, the evangelists, and the pastors and teachers. *Their responsibility is to equip God's people to do his work and build up the church*, the body of Christ" (emphasis added). Paul won't let us escape this truth. We have a responsibility to equip people to build the body of Christ. Most of us have no idea how to do that, which is why our attempts at evangelism languish.

Personal Evangelism

In the last section, you discovered how to use your church's stage, staff, and structure to create an environment that challenges your people to share their faith. Challenging them is essential, but it won't get you far if you aren't also equipping them for the challenge. So how do we give our members and regular attenders what they need to be able to invite their friends to church? What can we do to increase the likelihood that they will step out on faith and ask that often uncomfortable question? Personal evangelism is all about helping your people see the opportunities they have to invite their friends and then helping them seize those opportunities. You want them to *see* and *seize* every opening God provides.

Before we dive into the details of personal evangelism, let me be clear about one thing: our job is simply to share the gospel with as many people as possible. We cannot make unbelievers thirsty for God. That's the Holy Spirit's role. Remember what Jesus tells us in the book of John: "For no one can come to me unless the Father who sent me draws them to me" (6:44). God's Spirit is constantly at work in millions and millions of lives. He is creating a yearning in aching hearts that only he can fill. Every day our members and regular attenders walk in relationship with many of these yearning people. Our goal is to mobilize an evangelistic army that is ready and willing to point thirsty unbelievers toward the living water.

Finding the Right Formula

Getting your people ready for the work of evangelism is, well, work. You'll have to invest some time and effort. But if you commit to putting certain elements in place, you can ensure a heightened level of effectiveness. There is a proven way to grow the percentage of your people who are actually extending invitations at every opportunity. You just have to put what I call the "personal evangelism formula" to work for you. This formula looks like one you may remember from your algebra days. It follows the form of $x = a + b + c$. If x equals high levels of personal evangelism, let's take a closer look at the other elements we need to plug in to bring those high levels into being.

a = *Tools*. People are more likely to do what you ask of them if you give them some tools that will make things easier.

b = *Training*. They will respond even more favorably if you provide them with a little training so they feel confident in what they are being asked to do.

c = *Timeliness*. With tools and training, you will have your people on the right track, but there's one more thing that will greatly increase the likelihood that they'll start inviting people to church. Give them a reason to do it *now*. Provide a sense of urgency.

$$x = \text{Tools} + \text{Training} + \text{Timeliness}$$

That's the true formula for personal evangelism. If you give people the tools they need, train them on how to use those tools, and then give them a period of time in which they need to carry out their task, you will send your evangelistic temperature soaring.

High Levels of Personal Evangelism =
Tools + Training + Timeliness

Don't miss any of these three elements. Too often we train people from the stage or through small group studies, but we don't give them any accompanying tools. We don't put anything in their hands. Then again, sometimes we give them good tools and training but set no time frame. Successfully equipping our people means ensuring that we provide them with all three variables of the personal evangelism formula.

Recently, at The Journey, we put this formula to work for our fall big day. We were planning to kick off a sermon series called Financial Peace, based on Dave Ramsey's material, one month after school started back. Two weeks before the series was set to begin, we gave everyone in the congregation a stack of postcard invitations with the series information on one side and The Journey's location and meeting details on the other (tools). We briefly talked them through how to invite their friends to church (training) using the invitations. Take note that training your people doesn't mean putting them through a twelve-week personal evangelism course; it simply means taking a few minutes to walk them through how to use the tools you are providing to them. You can train in brief spurts from the stage on Sundays, through small groups, and in your membership classes. We'll go into more detail on tools and training in the next chapter.

We also encouraged our people to offer these Financial Peace invitations to their friends the next week (timeliness). As God had planned it, we were able to highlight the urgency of offering this invitation on a couple of levels. Not only was this exciting series about to kick off with a big day, but people were especially interested in finances at the time because of unusual market fluctuations. Around the city—and the world—people were concerned about their money. Fluctuating stocks were all over the news, and everyone was a little frightened. God positioned this series, which we had planned a year and a half earlier, to connect with people at a critical time. The urgency

90

for the series kickoff was inherently heightened. But that's not always the case, so you have to be able to create your own sense of urgency around your big days.

Creating Urgency

People do what's urgent. We operate not in the realm of the important but in the realm of the critical. In *The Seven Habits of Highly Effective People*, Stephen Covey writes, "Important matters that are not urgent require more initiative, more pro-activity."[2] While time management gurus like Covey encourage us to spend our lives focused on the important rather than the urgent, we need to make sure our personal evangelism opportunities cooperate with basic human nature. We don't want to ask our people to do anything that requires too much additional initiative or proactivity on their part. Instead, we should burn away such obstacles by igniting a fire of urgency around evangelism.

Think about your own life. I'm sure you are driven by deadlines. I know I am. You get ready for Sunday because it's always urgent. You pay the bills because there's an urgent need to keep the lights on. Perhaps it would be more important to have a heart-to-heart with a friend over a cup of coffee, but that can wait. It's important but not urgent. There are all kinds of things in your schedule that you do every day because they have to be done—even if they are not the most significant things you could be doing with your life. That's also true for every one of your members and regular attenders.

Lots of people have good intentions of inviting their friends to church, but those intentions live in the realm of the impor-

91

tant. They put it off until next Sunday and then the next. Why? Because they can. The service will still be there and the lights will still be on, so why not avoid a potentially awkward conversation for a little while longer? Many churchgoers rationalize evangelism away with this kind of thinking for years. But you can circumvent the procrastination by plugging urgency into your personal evangelism formula. Give your people a deadline for extending an invitation to their friends.

Big days create inherent urgency that you can capitalize on. For example, as you plan toward your February big day, you should start building the urgency week by week. A few Sundays out, begin telling your people frequently, "Invite your friends to the kickoff of our new series that's coming up." Then two weeks out, "Be sure to invite your friends to be here two weeks from now for our big series kickoff." Then, "Make sure you bring your friends with you next Sunday as we kick off our new series!" Palm Sunday is also a good urgency-inducing day. It gives you the opportunity to move away from general "just invite your friends" preaching to an "invite your friends to be here *next week* for Easter and the kickoff of our new series" push. When you add that element of urgency to the equation, you'll be amazed at what will happen. People will start taking the initiative to invite their friends. And one in four of those friends will show up for your big day from the first invitation. The key is learning to use urgency wisely, which leads me to the principle of stretch and release.

Stretch and Release

You may have already guessed that I am a big proponent of working with the natural realities that God built into us and our world. One of those realities is that we operate best within a pattern of stretch and release. We were created to work hard for six days and then rest for one. We go to school for nine months, then take three off. Our muscles develop during the rest periods between workouts. We are better suited for sprints than marathons. This cyclical truth is why we run our small groups at The Journey on a semester system. People grow more spiritually when they are encouraged to stretch themselves for a period of time and then have a break to rest. If we are constantly stretching, or stressing, we will burn out.

The principle of stretch and release says that people perform closest to their full potential when they are given periods of rest between stretches of growth. As you begin working to mobilize your people for evangelism, take this principle to heart. You can't stretch your members and regular attenders to do evangelism all the time. They will get tired of hearing you talk about it. They'll start to tune you out. If they haven't had success with evangelism in the past, they won't get the chance to recuperate and be ready to try again. The key is to stretch your people for a season—push them hard to invite their friends, provide them with tools, talk about it every Sunday—and then release. Let it rest.

Now, as I mentioned, at The Journey we say, "If you found today's message helpful, be sure to invite a friend to come with you next week," every week. We want to keep evangelism in the air. If new people are in the congregation, maybe they are ready to accept that challenge. For everyone else, we want to remind them that they should be ready to share their faith or invite someone to church whenever the opportunity arises. We encourage an evangelistic lifestyle every week, but we don't push people to be sharing their faith constantly. The reality is that they won't do it, and they'll burn out under the expectation. Instead, we create stretch benchmarks throughout the year. We do the big evangelistic pushes in cycles. In February, for Easter, and in September, we challenge and equip people to bring three friends. We stretch them, and then we give them a chance to breathe . . . and then we stretch them again. That's the natural ebb and flow God created; we're just taking advantage of his wisdom.

Church Leader Testimony

These ideas have helped us break growth barriers. Thanks to the principle of stretch and release, our people and leaders have been more motivated to learn and to come together to work on a common goal. We have had a 250 percent increase in first-time guests.

Mark Gregori, Lead Pastor
Crossway Church (Bronx, NY)

Personal evangelism is all about equipping your people to evangelize as they are called by God to do. Learning to create a sense of urgency several times a year will create the environment that is best suited to fulfilling that calling. But remember, urgency is just one of the variables in our personal evangelism formula. As you turn the heat up throughout the year, you have to make sure that your congregation has the training and the tools they need to be able to reach out to their friends confidently and effectively. It's a good thing that your people work best through stretch and release, because that release period gives you the perfect opportunity to equip them for the work they'll be doing when the urgency sets in.

8

equipping for evangelism

Little Tools That Make a Big Difference

The harvest is great, but the workers are few. So pray to the Lord who is in charge of the harvest; ask him to send more workers into his fields.

Luke 10:2

Nothing is to be expected from the workman whose tools are for ever to be sought.

Samuel Johnson

Open up your program again and find the little card that says 'Invest and Invite' at the top," Pastor Tim says as he starts winding down his message. He has just taught on evangelism in hopes of gearing people up to invite their friends to the big day, which is now three weeks away.

"You'll notice three lines on the back of that card. I'm going to give you just a minute right now, and I want you to write down the names of three people you may have been thinking of during the message," Tim continues. "These are the three people I want you to commit to inviting to the kickoff of our new series three weeks from today. . . . Take a minute and write the names God is putting on your heart."

Sam found his Invest and Invite card and clicked open his FCC pen. Without hesitating, he wrote "Jon and Liz" on the first line.

"Now," said Pastor Tim, drawing Sam's attention back to the stage, "as you leave today, you are going to receive a small stack of postcards. These postcards are to help you invite the people whose names you've just written down to come to church with you."

Sam was getting more excited by the minute. That's exactly what he had been needing—something solid that he could put in Jon's hand.

"They have information about the new series on one side and all of FCC's service details on the other," said Tim. "Let me remind you to be praying for the people on your list. Pray that God will be working in their lives so they'll be ready to accept your invitation. And then use these postcards as a tool when you invite them to come to church with you three Sundays from now."

Sam didn't hear much else that Tim said until, "See you next week." Then he was headed for the postcards in the back.

The right tools are essential to any job. Painters need brushes to paint. Builders need hammers to nail. Cooks need pans to sauté. You get the idea. In the same way, your members and regular attenders need tools to carry out the task of evangelism. Remember our personal evangelism formula from the last chapter:

High Levels of Personal Evangelism =
Tools + Training + Timeliness

In this equation, the tools and the training really go hand in hand. As you give people evangelistic tools and explain how to put them to use, you are training. Likewise, when you teach on evangelism from the stage, you are training—and in turn you should provide applicable tools. As you train, you will provide tools, and as you provide tools, you will train. Tools and training are the yin and yang of personal evangelism.

Tool Time

In encouraging the congregation of FCC to invite their friends to the upcoming big day, Pastor Tim hit on several effective tools you can provide to your people. Let's look at each one in more detail:

1. Have People Write Down the Names of Unchurched Friends

Habakkuk 2:2 tells us to "Write the vision and make it plain on tablets, that he may run who reads it" (NKJV). There is power in writing things down. When you preach on evangelism and then take the time to have people write down the names of friends who are on their hearts, they will be significantly more likely to see and seize opportunities to invite those people to church.

As we approach our Easter big day, I always use Palm Sunday to challenge our people to write down the names of ten unchurched friends they would like to invite to the Easter services. For most other big days, I challenge everyone a week or two in advance to write down the names of three unbelieving friends they will invite. This is also a great time to encourage members and regular attenders to continue making unchurched friends.

2. Lead People to Pray for the Unchurched

Earlier we learned that hearts are drawn to the people they pray for. One of the best ways to encourage personal evangelism is to lead people to pray for their unchurched friends and acquaintances. Pastor Tim used one of my favorite tools to get his people to both write down the names of those on their hearts and to remind them to pray for who they wrote down—the Invest and Invite card. At The Journey, an Invest and Invite card is simply a business card–sized card that says on one side, "I will seek to invest in others who don't have a personal relationship with Jesus Christ and invite them to The Journey." On the other side are three lines for our people to list the names of three friends they are committing to invest in and invite to church. We encourage everyone to keep this card alive throughout the year. If one of the friends on the list moves away, we want them to add another friend's name. As part of the challenge I mentioned above, I lead people to fill out new Invest and Invite cards a few weeks before every big day. (See appendix 3 for Invest and Invite card samples. To download the cards, visit www.ignitebook.com.)

3. Utilize Invitation Cards

Provide your people with something they can hand to their friends when they extend the invitation. An invitation card can take many forms, as long as it contains all of the pertinent information about your services. Like Pastor Tim's cards, invitation cards can simply be postcards that advertise your upcoming series on one side and give details about the church's location and meeting times on the other side. At The Journey, we create these postcards for every new series—they are our most effective and consistent invitation tool. In the weeks before kicking off a new series, we give stacks of five to ten postcards to our members and regular attenders after each service, in conjunction with having them write down the names of and pray for their unchurched friends. As we all know, everything (in evangelism) works together for good. (For more examples of The Journey's invitation cards, see www.ignitebook.com.)

We've also been known to get creative with invitation cards at The Journey. One of the most effective things we've done is to create a small, foldable card that has the New York City subway map on the inside. Our people keep a few of those in their pockets or purses, and when the opportunity arises, they have a great tool for inviting someone in the city to The Journey. If they see someone looking at a station subway map, they can offer the card. If someone needs directions somewhere, they can offer the card. Or they can offer the card as part of any conversation and say, "Hey, hold on to that. It's pretty useful. There's a subway map inside." We have been able to give away close to two million invitations thanks to those subway maps.

Think about your culture. What is something that people in your community would be interested in receiving and holding on to that could also serve as an invitation to your church? Maybe a bus schedule or a train schedule? How about the high school football team's season schedule? Just print the schedule on one side and the information about your church on the other. You could position yourself at the team's home opener and hand those to everyone coming in. The possibilities are vast. Just keep it small, so that people can always have a few tucked away, and make sure to include all of the relevant information.

Church Leader Testimony

We have become more intentional in praying for and inviting people to our church. One of the things we've incorporated has been to distribute invite cards. Almost immediately we began to see an increase in first-time guests. In fact, over 75 percent of our first-time guests say they came because of the personal invite.

Terry Mahan, Lead Pastor
The Father's House Christian Center (Leesburg, FL)

4. Encourage Everyone in Entry-Level Evangelism

Remember the FCC pen that Sam used to write down Jon's and Liz's names? Pens with your church's information printed on them can be extremely powerful evangelism tools. Each Sunday at The Journey, everyone gets a Journey pen with their program. Since we use fill-in-the-blank message notes, we don't want to leave anyone without a pen. From time to time, I like to have some fun and truly turn those pens into a tool. Toward the end of the service, I will say, "How many of you have more than five Journey pens at home?" Almost everyone raises their hands, because they all take the pens home every week. Then I challenge them, "Why not make it a goal to give those pens away this week? Give one to a friend. Use one to sign your receipt at a restaurant and leave it on the table." People who may not be comfortable inviting a friend to church will probably be comfortable offering a pen to that friend. The pens give everyone the opportunity to take a small step toward evangelism. And you would be amazed how well these pens evangelize. At least once a month, we hear from someone who came to our church for the first time because of a Journey pen.

My favorite type of entry-level evangelism is servant evangelism. My friend and mentor Steve Sjogren introduced the concept in his book *Conspiracy of Kindness*. Over the years, I have come to define servant evangelism as sharing the love and message of Jesus Christ through practical acts of service and kindness. Servant evangelism is a biblical, fun, simple, and intentional way to make sharing Jesus a lifestyle. It's also a form of evangelism that anyone can participate in. The truth is that only about 5 percent of the people in our churches have the gift of direct evangelism—the ability to sit across a table from an unbeliever and share their faith. But 95 percent of churchgoers can invite their friends to church and reach out to the community through servant evangelism projects. And they will, as you give them the encouragement and opportunity to do so.

Church Leader Testimony

Recently our church held a servant evangelism outreach to demonstrate the love of Christ in an extremely practical way by serving the felt needs of the community. We organized a "Gas Buy Down" at three separate gas stations throughout our area. A "Gas Buy Down" is when a local church pays a gas station to lower the price of gas over a set period of time for customers in the community. Fifty volunteers showed up on the day of the outreach, which was timed for two weeks prior to the kickoff of a brand-new sermon series on relationships. We distributed invitations to the new series and other items to help people grow in their faith journey. Overall, the event was a major success. We purchased four thousand gallons of gas and shared the love of Christ in word and deed with hundreds of people in our community. On the day of the new sermon series kickoff, we broke the one thousand barrier. Three families who attended the church for the first time as a result of the "Gas Buy Down" and the big day two weeks later were recently baptized. It is amazing how far a little kindness goes in a world that is full of hurt.

David Crosby, Senior Pastor
Pocono Community Church (Mount Pocono, PA)

At The Journey, we provide lots of opportunities for our people to get involved in servant evangelism. For many of our regular attenders and members, their first exposure comes through a small group. As I detail in *Activate: An Entirely New Approach to Small Groups*, we schedule each of our small groups to participate in one servant evangelism project together during the semester. Often we will host a "Servant Evangelism Saturday" in a busy part of town and invite different groups to participate. Once someone has ventured into servant evangelism as part of a small group experience, they are more likely to get connected with other outreach opportunities that come up throughout the year—both personal and corporate. (For an overview of servant evangelism and a strategy for leading a Servant Evangelism Saturday, see appendix 4 and appendix 5. Visit www.ignitebook .com for a copy of my bestselling resource entitled "How to Reach Your Community through Servant Evangelism.")

5. Encourage Friend and Family Invites

Pastor Tim didn't mention this one, but utilize your special events to encourage friend and family invitations. For example, when you do a baby dedication, make sure that all of the parents invite their friends and family to church that day. Many people who wouldn't be open to coming to church through a regular invitation will come because a niece or grandson is being dedicated. Or they will come because their co-worker is giving a testimony on a Sunday morning and they are curious to hear what he says. They'll come because their friend from college is singing a solo or because their son is being baptized. Encourage your people to take advantage of any and every special opportunity to extend invitations to their difficult-to-reach friends and family.

At The Journey, we like to take this encouragement a step further and actually equip people to invite friends and family to their special day. About a month before each baptism service, we provide people who are being baptized with invitation cards that say, "You are invited to my baptism." The cards contain all of the pertinent date, time, and location information. Then, at the baptism celebration, we present the gospel in a simple, nonthreatening way. We want everyone there to understand the decision that those being baptized are making and have the opportunity to make that decision themselves. I believe so strongly in promoting baptisms, child dedications, and the like that I tend to turn them into "mini big days"—a simple tweak that brings lots of rewards.

Expectation and Celebration

When you ask your people to invite their friends to church, you are asking them to trust you. To feel confident in extending an

103

invitation to those closest to them, people have to know that they can count on the service being well-organized and the preaching being strong. They want to know that the worship team is going to be good. In short, they have to know what to expect. If they come to church week after week and find inconsistencies in the service, you'll be hard-pressed to convince them to invite their friends. The moment they do, they are linking their reputation to yours. Prove to them what they can expect through your consistent excellence, and then come through on the Sunday that their elusive neighbor finally decides to show up.

And when that neighbor shows up, celebrate! Psychologists tell us that what gets rewarded gets repeated. When someone brings a guest, celebrate with him. If you know about it right away, thank him after the service. Share evangelism stories. Highlight the value that you place on people who bring people. One way to do that is to offer an immediate reward incentive. Every summer at The Journey, we do a series called "God on Film." The week before the kickoff, I always tell people that if they bring a guest to church the next week, I will give both them and their guest a free movie ticket. And we always have a lot of guests! Of course you can't do that all the time, but once or twice a year gives people a little extra push to make the big ask of their friends. When evangelism is appreciated and celebrated, people want to be a part of it.

In the spirit of this celebration, I make a habit of sending handwritten thank-you notes to people who bring a friend to a service with them. Each week I get the names of those who invited our first-time guests. I pull these from the "How did you hear about The Journey?" question on our Connection Cards and from pastors and staff who happened to meet first-time guests and the friend who brought them. Then I write a note, thanking that person for living out their faith by inviting a friend to church. Usually I include a $10 Starbucks card and encourage the person to grab a cup of coffee with the friend to get a sense of what they thought of the experience. Our people appreciate knowing that we are not only paying attention but also rewarding them for their willingness to reach out.

As you begin to put the personal evangelism formula to work in your church, make sure you are focusing on all three elements—training, tools, and timeliness. You and I have a command and an obligation to equip our members and regular attenders to be strong workers in the field. The more thoroughly we prepare them, the better job they will do, and the greater harvest we will reap.

promotion

9

finding fertile ground

The Art of Choosing Wisely

Listen! A farmer went out to plant some seed . . .

Mark 4:3

One of the major barriers to church growth is "people blindness."

Rick Warren

You may have heard the old story about the science professor who set out to prove a point to a class of sleepy freshmen. One morning he placed a large, empty glass vase on his desk, and with the students paying little attention, he filled the vase with medium-sized stones. He put the stones in one by one until the vase couldn't hold any more. Then he asked his students, "Is this vase full?" They half-nodded their assertion that it was.

The professor pulled a bucket of pebbles from under his desk. Slowly he poured the pebbles into the vase. They bounced and settled into the small spaces that had been created between the stones. Once again the professor asked his students, who were now slightly more awake, "Is this vase full?" They all quietly contended that, yes, of course it was.

The professor proceeded to pull another bucket from beneath his desk—this one filled with fine sand. As the students looked on, he tilted the bucket of sand into the vase. The granules quickly filled in the barely visible cracks and crevices left between the stones and pebbles. This time when asked, "Is this vase full?" the class answered with a resounding "Yes!" Every inch of the vase was taken. There was no space for anything else.

In response to his students' certainty, the professor reached under his desk and brought out a pitcher of water. The freshmen watched in amazement as the professor poured the entire pitcher into the vase, where the water soaked into the sand and solidified all of the previously invisible remaining space. "Now," the professor said to his students, "this vase is full."

Filling the Gaps

Personal evangelism is the single most effective way to bring new people to your church—but it's not enough. No matter how well you train your people, how timely you make the message, or what kind of tools you give them, you will never be able to reach everyone in your community through person-to-person evangelism. The numbers won't work. Think about the size of your church in relation to your community. How long would it take to evangelize your entire area, even if you were able to get every single one of your people to bring four friends to church each year?

The Journey is a relatively large church in the middle of New York. God has allowed us to reach and disciple many hundreds of unchurched people. The only problem is that there are close to eight million people in the greater New York City area who need Jesus. If we, as a church, decided to rely solely on personal evangelism, we would be choosing to leave gaping holes in our strategy. As would you. There is room for so much more.

Think of your evangelism system as the glass vase on that professor's desk. Personal evangelism outreaches are like the medium-sized stones that went in first. They are the most effective way of filling the vase, but they can't complete the job on their own. They need to be surrounded and supported by something else. That something else is mass promotion. The various methods of mass promotion that you disperse into your community are like the pebbles, sand, and water the professor used in his example. They cover the inevitable holes in your personal evangelism efforts and make your system complete— or full, if you will.

In working with churches and leaders across the country, I've run into a surprisingly high number of people who think that personal evangelism on its own is enough to keep the evangelistic temperature hot. They have decided to focus on person-to-person invitations as their single method of outreach. These leaders remind me of the students who thought that the vase was full after the professor put in the medium-sized stones. They are choosing not to look at the spaces that are left around those stones—spaces that, if filled, would give them much greater influence in the community and would result in many more first-time guests.

Granted, the return on mass marketing campaigns is not as high as the return on personal invitations. It may take two thousand fliers going out into the community to get one person to come to your church, especially if your personal evangelism and promotion are not working in concert with each other. The key is to get them working together. Be as intentional about promotion as you are about personal evangelism, and make sure that one complements the other. Then God will cause your promotion efforts to maximize your congregation's personal evangelism efforts in amazing ways. You will not only reach new people but also ignite your personal evangelism effectiveness.

Experience has taught me that there is a true spiritual connection between personal evangelism and promotion when both are being done correctly and with the right heart. I can't tell you how many times I have been on a street corner doing servant evangelism and had someone say to me, as I hand off a granola bar and an invitation to church, "You know, you handed one of these cards to a friend of mine last week. I have been trying to get him to church for months. Thanks for backing me up like this." That is not a coincidence. We are talking about street corners in the middle of New York City. Hundreds of people are coming and going with every change of the crosswalk sign. The chances of my ten-minute evangelistic outreach falling into the hands of someone already being invited to church by one of my attenders surpasses any kind of human planning. God definitely works through our efforts to reach people for his glory.

One more thing about that glass vase: just picture how much sturdier the medium-sized stones became once they were wedged a little tighter by the pebbles. And think about how solidly the stones and the pebbles were made to fit together when encompassed by the sand. By the time the water filled the vase to the brim, those first stones were locked in, supported on every side. That's how your people feel when you surround them with promotion to help their personal evangelism efforts. You are providing air cover for them. By putting your church's name into the community, you are making it easier for them to invite their friends. The more mass promotion you pour into your area, the more supported they will feel—and the more likely they will be to reach out.

Church Leader Testimony

We have chosen to frame the evangelism concepts in military terms: employing the "air support" through a number of different advertising media, then firing up and sending out the "infantry" in the form of personal invitations. Implementing this evangelism system strategy provides us with a great opportunity to get more people involved in the process.

Tommy Duke, Lead Pastor
Iron City Church (Pittsburgh, PA)

The Sower and the Seed

Let's take a look at Jesus's words in Mark 4:3–9:

> "Listen! A farmer went out to plant some seed. As he scattered it across his field, some of the seed fell on a footpath, and the birds came and ate it. Other seed fell on shallow soil with underlying rock. The seed sprouted quickly because the soil was shallow. But the plant soon wilted under the hot sun, and since it didn't

have deep roots, it died. Other seed fell among thorns that grew up and choked out the tender plants so they produced no grain. Still other seeds fell on fertile soil, and they sprouted, grew, and produced a crop that was thirty, sixty, and even a hundred times as much as had been planted!" Then he said, "Anyone with ears to hear should listen and understand."

The parable of the sower and the seed gives us great insight into the idea of promotion. We can draw a lot of truth from the wisdom of the story's main character. One inherent fact that Jesus doesn't state specifically but that we can infer is that this wise farmer was sowing his seed at the right time of year. If we know that some of the seed fell on fertile ground, sprouted, and grew, then he was obviously sowing the seed when it needed to be sown. We've already discussed the power of intentional timing. A wise church leader sows in January to reap a harvest in February. He sows on Palm Sunday to reap on Easter. And he sows the month school starts back to reap a big crop the month after things are in full swing.

Once we recognize the importance of when to sow our seed, we are ready for the first principle Jesus wants to teach us through the wise farmer: *pinpoint your best fields*. In order to sow effectively, you have to know what fields to scatter your seed in. You have to identify and concentrate on the most fertile soil and use seed that will take root there. Otherwise your efforts will be in vain. To identify your best fields, ask yourself these questions:

1. Who Am I Currently Reaching?

If God is predominantly bringing a certain type of person to your church, that's a good indicator of who you are most equipped to reach. A couple of years ago, the average age of Journey attenders was twenty-seven. That has increased a little now, but we've always had a special outreach with the late twentysomethings. So we focused our seed-sowing on soil that would reach that group. We created invitations that would be appealing to them. We thought about how we could connect with them in their current reality. This led to one of my favorite invitation projects in our history.

In thinking about how to reach these twentysomethings, the first question we asked ourselves was, "Where can we find them? Where do they hang out en masse?" The best answer? In the Greenwich Village bars on Friday nights. Now, in New York City, you aren't allowed to smoke inside—and a lot of young New Yorkers are smokers. This meant that all of these people who perfectly fit The Journey's target demographic were hanging out on street corners, smoking cigarettes, just waiting for me—a wise farmer—to walk by and hand them a seed. Can you guess what we handed them? Matchbooks with an invitation to The Journey printed on the flap. We ordered five thousand boxes of matchbooks and hit the Village, armed and ready to reach more people like the ones God was already bringing us.

2. Who Is Like Me?

You are best equipped to reach people who are like you. That's a fact of human nature. You will attract who you are. In *The Purpose-Driven Church*, Rick Warren asserts, "If you are a pastor, you must honestly ask yourself, 'What kind of person am I? What is my cultural background? What kind of people do I naturally relate to and what kind do I have a harder time understanding?' You need to do a frank analysis of who you are and the type of people to whom you relate best."[1]

3. Who Is Not Churched?

Your best fields are in the middle of the unchurched. If some of your promotion falls into the hands of Christians involved in other churches, so be it. But current Christians should not be your target. Instead, keep your attention focused on those who are unchurched in your community. God is working in their lives. Concentrate on pointing them toward his hope.

If you aren't sure how to begin outreach to the unchurched, start by focusing on people who are under tension, undergoing transition, or in trouble. Time and time again, I have found that people are most open to hearing the truth of the gospel when God has them in one of these three situations. That's one of the reasons that a relationship series works so well in February. People are often under tension, undergoing transition, or in trouble relationally during that time of the year.

Understanding these three Ts—tension, transition, and trouble—will exponentially increase your effectiveness in the unchurched world. In fact, let me encourage you to do an exercise that will help you focus in on the types of situations that the people around you are dealing with. Pull the key leaders in your church together and talk through the greatest tensions and trouble they see in the lives of those they live around every day. Ask them to think about what kind of transitions they see people facing. Sketch all of these down and then begin planning outreach that will connect with those experiencing such tension, transition, and trouble. Think about planning a big day kickoff sermon around the greatest felt need that comes up in your discussion.

Step outside of the box here. Evangelizing people who are moving into your community works well, because they are undergoing transition. If the economy is suffering and people are losing jobs, many of them become open to the gospel for the first time because of the tension they are under. Stay attuned to what's going on in the lives of the unchurched in your community and meet them where they are.

Church Leader Testimony

During the financial crisis, we were able to do a servant evangelism event for stock brokers. We served breakfast at a local office where a couple of our members work. We provided everyone in the office with a free copy of The Purpose-Driven Life *and gave each of them a personal, handwritten card to let them know that we would be praying for them during the difficult period. Then, in our staff meeting later that day, we prayed for every worker and his or her family. Over the next couple of weeks, people kept stopping me around town to say, "Thank you. You will never know the impact that had on our office." We were able to touch thirty people who were hurting and facing tough times.*

Marty Martin
Northstar Church (Panama City, FL)

Birds, Sun, and Thorns

Notice that the wise farmer in our parable loses quite a bit of his seed in bad fields. As he sows, the birds come in and eat some of the seed. The sun beams down and scorches other seed.

And even seed that starts to sprout gets cut off in its infancy by those pesky thorns. Yet the farmer keeps sowing. Jesus doesn't tell us that the farmer takes a rake and shoos the birds away or that he stands shaking his fist at the sun. No, he keeps sowing, knowing that the results were up to God.

In my early days of ministry, I had a problem with getting caught up in the bad fields. I was constantly bemoaning and putting down the fields that wouldn't produce a crop. I spent a lot of time trying to identify the birds and get rid of them. I would sow seed on what I thought was fertile soil and the sun, with all its intense pressure, would come and dry the crop up. I would see people start to grow and then grope around in despair when the thorns came in and strangled them. I just couldn't understand why the birds, the sun, and the thorns had such an impact on my evangelistic efforts.

Over the years, God has taught me not to focus on the seed that falls on infertile soil or the seed that gets eaten by the birds, burned by the sun, or choked by the thorns. My job—and yours—is not to figure out how to get rid of those things but to sow our seeds of evangelism in the best fields possible and leave the results up to God. In the passage, Jesus tells us, "Anyone with ears to hear should listen and understand" (Mark 4:9). This means understanding the reality of the forces that will work against us, not pulling our hair out trying to change the course of nature that God has set in place.

God calls us to focus on the fertile soil. The enemy is always going to be working against our efforts to bring people into the knowledge of Jesus Christ. If we get caught up in what the enemy is doing, we lose our clarity on what God wants to do. But if we pour ourselves into spreading seeds of promotion throughout our communities—supporting the stones in that vase with pebbles, sand, and water—we will reap the harvest in due time. God will work through our offering, grow everything that falls on fertile ground, and infuse our evangelistic outreach with his power.

10

sowing the best seed

And Trusting God for Big Results

Live wisely among those who are not believers, and make the
most of every opportunity.

the apostle Paul (Colossians 4:5)

We plough the fields and scatter
The good seed on the land,
But it is fed and watered
By God's almighty hand.

Matthias Claudius

Finally, Saturday. Jon strains one eye to see the clock on his
dresser: 8:30. With a sigh, he throws back the covers and
slowly rolls out of bed. He can hear Liz and the kids making
breakfast downstairs. As Jon heads slowly toward the bathroom,

he wonders why Saturdays don't feel as free to him as they once did. Admittedly, he's been worried about what's going on at the bank. They've had several layoffs in the last couple of weeks. "But surely that's not what's weighing on me today," Jon thinks to himself. "I'm pretty secure."

After brushing his teeth and sliding into his favorite alma mater sweatpants, Jon heads downstairs.

"Good morning, Daddy!" Madison and Johnny shout in unison. Well, almost.

"Good morning, sleepy head," Liz says.

"Yeah, sorry. I just didn't feel like getting up this morning," Jon says, heading for the coffeemaker. "Where's the paper?"

"It's on the table outside," answers Liz. "I was reading it before they got up. Not great news."

Coffee in hand, Jon heads to the porch. He sits down and closes his eyes. He hears birds chirping, a neighbor's lawn mower humming in the distance, his children's voices floating out from the kitchen . . . and wonders why he isn't any happier.

Jon picks up the front page and reads the headline: MORE BANKS IN TROUBLE AS MARKET CONTINUES TO TUMBLE. The gnawing feeling that's becoming all too familiar to him lately creeps into his gut. He takes a sip of coffee and a deep breath.

Trying to find some positive news, Jon starts flipping through the Living section, where a full-page, color ad catches his eye. "Does God care about your financial security?" asks the ad. "Discover how to live in financial peace, this Sunday at FCC," it continues. Jon stares at the page, trying to figure out why FCC sounds familiar to him. Then it hits. That's the church that Sam, the guy in the office next to his at the bank, has been trying to get him to for a couple of months. He has been able to come up with a good excuse for not being able to make it every time so far, but he's beginning to run out.

Jon looks back to the ad. "Does God care about my financial security?" he lets himself wonder. "Probably not."

Liz steps onto the porch and catches a glimpse of the ad over Jon's shoulder. "What's that?" she asks.

Think back to Jesus's parable of the sower and the seed. Mark 4 tells us that the wise farmer scattered his seed across the field. He covered every corner in hopes of reaping the greatest possible harvest. He sowed seed generously and left the results up to God. If we hope to truly ignite evangelism in our churches, we need to take another lesson from that farmer and decide to *plant the maximum number of seeds possible.* No matter what kind of promotion we are considering, we must get in the habit of thinking big.

Do you think the farmer scattered only a little of his seed or all that he had? Of course he scattered all he had. He didn't leave any reserves back in the storehouse but rather trusted God to provide as he did what he'd been called to do. Even though the farmer knew that some of the seed would fall on bad ground, he still scattered it. He understood that he was investing in the great return that the harvest would bring.

Investing in Seed

Before we get into the details of promotion, let me challenge your thinking a bit. I want to ensure that you see the money required to do promotion as an investment, because that's exactly what it is. God honors our money when we pour it into reaching more people for the kingdom. We should never think of promotion as an expense. God taught me this lesson in no uncertain terms several years ago. At the time, The Journey had been in existence for about three years. I had called a big meeting to talk about our summer outreach to the unchurched in our community. I was about to walk into that meeting knowing that we were planning to make a decision to do 168,000 servant evangelism touches over the course of the summer. At just over $0.20 per touch, that would have been an investment of roughly $35,000.

We had a slight problem: we only had $30,000 in the bank. Sitting in my office before the meeting, I wrestled with myself and God. I started thinking that maybe we should do only 80,000 touches. We would probably still see some results and wouldn't go broke in the meantime. Just as I was about to head into the meeting and put forth this very proposal, my phone rang. I picked it up to hear a pastor friend of mine from a small town in Virginia on the other end. This friend's county had a population of about six thousand people, and he had grown a church of two thousand. Here's how our conversation played out after the initial chitchat:

"Nelson, I'm concerned that we aren't reaching enough people in the community," said Jimmie.

I said, "There are only six thousand in your whole county and two thousand of them go to your church. That's great. You are reaching people, man. You are reaching people."

"No," he said, "I really need to talk to you about some of the stuff we are doing."

At first I thought about asking him if I could call him back because I was about to walk into the evangelism meeting, but something kept me on the phone. "What do you want to talk about?" I asked.

"Well," Jimmie said, "I really wanted to talk to you about this passage of Scripture—2 Corinthians 9:10."

"What do you mean?" I asked, checking my watch. "What about the passage?"

"In that Scripture, God gives seed to the sower. . . . I've just been thinking. I don't know if we are being intentional and risky enough when it comes to putting it all on the line to reach people."

I quickly looked up the passage: "For God is the one who provides seed for the farmer and then bread to eat. In the same way, he will provide and increase your resources and then pro-duce a great harvest of generosity in you" (2 Cor. 9:10).

Talk about being convicted. There I was, sitting in the mid-dle of Manhattan with two thousand people within a stone's throw, and I was about to make a decision to cut our evange-listic ministry for the summer in half. Meanwhile, my friend was in a town where it's hard to count six thousand—with two thousand of them in his church—and he's burdened about reaching people.

Thanks to Jimmie's timely call, I walked into that evange-lism meeting with a new boldness. I determined that we were going to do those 168,000 touches over the next two months. That was June. Over the next eight weeks, we spent $35,000 on evangelism. Guess how much money we had in the bank in September? We had $35,000. That's God math. We started with $30,000, spent $35,000 on evangelism, and ended up with $35,000. God proved to me, in a tangible way, how he wants to bless those who are willing to step out in faith in an effort to reach people for him. I challenge you, as you think about what kind of promotional outreach you can do: don't let money be the determining factor. Think big. Ask God what he wants you to do, despite the cost, and then trust him to provide.

Planting Promotional Seeds

As you start to think about the kind of promotion you'd like to put into your community, keep your culture in mind. Just because a certain type of promotion works well in Chicago doesn't mean the same thing will be effective in Louisville. You need to know your community and gear your promotion in a way that will resonate with its people. Also remember that different kinds of bait will catch different kinds of fish, so to speak. As Rick Warren writes, "I've noticed that whenever I go fishing, the fish don't automatically jump into my boat or throw themselves up onto the shore for me. Their culture (underwater) is very different from mine (air). It takes intentional effort on my part to make contact with the fish. Somehow I must figure out how to get the bait right in front of their nose in their culture."[1]

Before you launch a promotional campaign, think about the type of "fish" in your community and what type of "bait" is best suited to catch them. In other words, what kind of seed is best suited to produce the desired crop? Here are four examples of promotional seed that work well in most areas:

1. **Direct mail**—Do you get postcards in your mailbox inviting you to churches in the area? If not, you should give direct mail a try. When people aren't already being inundated with church mailers, good promotional pieces

delivered directly into community mailboxes can be very effective. If you decide to do direct mail, don't skimp. Mail to as many key zip codes as you possibly can. Blanket your community in mailers so that everyone who is being invited to your church by one of your regular attenders has a good shot at receiving a direct mailer too. (For examples of direct mail promotion, see www .ignitebook.com.)

2. **Newspaper and radio advertising**—As we saw with Jon, newspaper advertising is a good way to connect with people where they are. The members of your community are reading the newspaper. Usually it is causing them to think about the state of the world and the state of their lives. A catchy ad or insert will grab people's attention.

If done professionally, radio advertising can also be effective. One of the riskiest promotional campaigns we ever did was through radio advertising. Earlier I mentioned the brainstorming session I had a while back with some key leaders on my staff—the one where I threw out that question I like to consider from time to time: "What is the riskiest thing we could do to reach people? What would really make the devil mad?" We decided that it would be a big step for us to advertise on the radio. So the next question was how to position the ad. Well, again, our target demographic was late-twentysomethings. We decided to look at reality in designing our bait. What do late-twentysomething, single guys listen to on the radio? *The Howard Stern Show.* So, as you'll remember, we decided to run an ad for The Journey on Howard Stern's morning show. Here's the rest of the story, and how we were able to use the ad as both promotion and personal evangelism.

To stay within our budget for the project, we signed a deal for thirty ads—only one of which would definitely hit at 8:30 a.m. during the week before our new series kickoff. The placement of the other twenty-nine were at the radio station's discretion. The campaign worked wonders. We generated more buzz for The Journey through that promotion than through anything before or since. The risk factor pushed people to talk to their friends about the church. All around the city, people were telling their acquaintances and co-workers, "Hey, my church is advertising on Howard Stern next week." The promotion complemented and encouraged person-to-person evangelism and at the same time reached a whole new segment of our target audience. Yes, it was risky, but it paid off in a big way.

3. Servant evangelism—As we've discussed, servant evangelism is an extremely effective way of promoting your church while meeting a practical need of the people in your community. Servant evangelism projects help your regular attenders and members get more comfortable with sharing their faith while canvassing the community with seed. Sometimes big servant evangelism projects even attract the positive interest of the local media, which is an added bonus. In my book, it is win-win promotion.

Church Leader Testimony

We decided to do a servant evangelism project through a "Gas Buy Down." Our primary goal was to show God's love to a lot of folks in a simple way. What we had not planned on was the secondary perk of advertising. When I arrived at the gas station thirty minutes early, a popular field reporter from one of the Cincinnati television networks was already on-site with a mobile broadcasting unit. Not long after we began, the only network helicopter in Cincinnati appeared in the sky. We were featured on three of the four Cincinnati networks over a two-hour period. In total, we had over nine minutes of network advertising during the five o'clock news slots. Best of all, there were families in our worship service the next Sunday who said they heard about us through the "Gas Buy Down."

Mike Osborne, Lead Pastor
Journey: A Community of Faith
(Union, KY/Greater Cincinnati)

4. **Billboard advertising**—A well-placed billboard promotion puts your church in front of the community and gets people talking. Just imagine the power of a prominent billboard on the main highway that your people travel to work and school. When they are in a car with their unchurched friends, they can easily use the billboard to open a conversation: "Hey, look, that's my church right there." Billboards also underscore and help validate an invitation that someone may have received earlier that day from a friend. Such well-placed, obvious promotion supports your people in their personal evangelism efforts.

I have seen these four types of promotional seed work well in many different environments, but they are certainly not the only promotions you can do. Again, think about your culture and don't be afraid to step outside of the box. I've worked with leaders who have promoted through cinema ads, trade show advertising, door hangers, floats in the community parade, television commercials, welcome wagon fliers for new residents, and the ticker tape at the DMV. The possibilities are virtually endless. As long as you are supporting your congregation's personal evangelism outreaches and offering clear invitations to your church, you can't go wrong. If you haven't done much promotion in the past, I encourage you to try something. Just pick one approach and give it a shot.

As you promote your church, I challenge you to think exponentially. Think big. In the same way that Jimmie challenged me to trust God to provide seed for my servant evangelism outreach, let me challenge you to trust God to reach more people than ever before through your evangelism efforts. Maybe you've been thinking about doing a ten-thousand-piece mailer. Why not stretch your faith and do a *hundred*-thousand-piece mailer? Or hit the same ten thousand homes three times, since most direct mail experts say that hitting a home only once is a waste of time. Maybe you've been planning to blanket three neighborhoods with door hangers about your church. Why not make it thirteen neighborhoods . . . or thirty? Take your current promotion number and add a zero. Let God stretch you for the sake of reaching as many people as possible as quickly as possible. After all, the return of Jesus is imminent, right? This is urgent. So remember, always plant the maximum number of seeds possible.

About Seeds

The farmer in Jesus's parable knew a lot about the nature of seeds. As we've seen, he knew how to pinpoint the best fields for planting, and he knew to plant the maximum number of seeds that he could. But that's not where his insight stopped. The farmer also understood what to do once the seed had been scattered. He knew to *expect a proportional return*, and he worked knowing that he would have to *wait for the coming harvest*.

When you are dealing with promotion, understand that you are never going to get a one-to-one ratio of return. Don't expect to, or you will be disappointed. You won't mail one postcard and get one first-time guest. You'll have to mail tens of thousands of postcards. Think of it as tilling the ground to keep the soil fertile. Then, as I mentioned, don't focus on the promotion that falls to the birds, gets scorched by the sun, or gets choked by the thorns. Focus instead on the return that you do get. And always keep sowing more seed, even as you wait for the coming harvest.

Farmers live with the principle of delayed gratification every day. Once the seed falls onto fertile soil, there is a waiting period before the harvest. Sometimes you will do a massive promotion and it will be weeks, months, or even years before you see the resulting harvest. You have to trust that God is watering those seeds in the fertile soil and that they will sprout when he intends.

Recently I met a young woman in our church who received a servant evangelism touch on Wall Street over four years ago. She told me that she had held on to that postcard for four years. She had never been able to bring herself to throw it away. And then one day the Spirit prompted her to go to church. So she pulled out the postcard and came to The Journey. Here's a question to consider: when the Spirit of God prompts someone in your community to attend church for the first time, where will she go? Will she know about your church? Will God lead her through your doors because you've cooperated with him in doing the work of promotion? Think big, plant your seeds, and wait. The harvest will come in due time.

11

reaping the harvest

The Keys to Effective Promotion

The seed that fell on good soil represents those who truly hear and understand God's word and produce a harvest of thirty, sixty, or even a hundred times as much as had been planted!

Matthew 13:23

I will prepare . . . and my chance will come.

Abraham Lincoln

Waiting is not an easy thing to do. In our "get it now" generation, we are accustomed to immediate results. With the click of a button, we can connect with people all over the world instantaneously. We can send a letter three thousand miles with the guarantee that it will be in the recipient's hands within hours. We can buy the fast pass at Disney World and zip to the front of every line as we teach our children that they too have evolved past having to wait for good things.

The concept of waiting for a harvest may be a little difficult for some of us to stomach, given our culture. But think once again of that wise farmer. He knew when he scattered his seed that it would be months before he saw any return. Do you think he paced and fretted and checked for results every day? Of course not. That would have been a monstrous waste of time. He understood that his crop would come in the time frame that had been determined by God. So he waited—patiently. But he did something while he waited. He used the time to *prepare and plan for the future.*

Mark 4 tells us that the seed the farmer scattered "produced a crop that was thirty, sixty, and even a hundred times as much as had been planted" (v. 8). We can be sure that the farmer knew what kind of harvest was in store. He had seen God multiply his seed many times before. But do you think he kicked his feet up after planting and said, "My part's finished, God. Your turn. Just bring the harvest and then I'll figure out what to do with it"? No way. While the farmer waited, he prepared and planned for what was to come.

When you make the decision to couple personal evangelism and promotion, you'd better prepare for the harvest that God wants to bring. If you fail to prepare for the blessing, he probably won't reveal it. Why would he? If you aren't prepared to shepherd the unchurched people who may come to you as a result of your evangelistic outreach, why would God put them under your care? He would prefer to send them to the church that is prepared to clear the way for them to meet him.

The principle of spiritual readiness tells us that God will never give us more than we are prepared to receive. I can't fully explain why this principle holds true, but I've seen it in action many times over. Your level of preparation is directly linked to the number of people God will send to your church. If you don't prepare while you are waiting for the harvest, you are essentially undercutting the future crop that God wants to bring you. You need to have a plan in place that will remove any stumbling blocks that could keep those new people from meeting God and becoming fully developing followers of Jesus. God has given every single one of us a responsibility and a commission to prepare for the harvest. And he knows full well whether or not you are creating an environment where he will be free to work. He will bless your evangelistic outreach accordingly.

One time I was planning to do an evangelism push at The Journey that involved a free gift. I told our congregation that I was going to give a gift—a new book I had been recommending—to everyone who brought a friend with them the next week. In preparation, we went out and bought two hundred of the books. Guess how many guests we had? One hundred eighty-six. What if we had only bought one hundred books? I venture to say that we would have had less than one hundred guests. On the other hand, what if we had bought four hundred books? I'm convinced that God would have brought us even more first timers. I've seen this kind of scenario play out at The Journey and in other churches many times. We prepare and plan—and then trust that God will bring the increase.

It's Friday afternoon. Sam sits at his desk, staring at the FCC invitation card he brought to work with him. He's nervous. In the past, he has swallowed the nerves that tried to keep him from inviting Jon to church, but he's beginning to get embarrassed. How many times does he have to be told no? Jon seems so busy. There's always a reason he can't make it to FCC.

Still, Sam can't shake the sense that he needs to put his own feelings and fears aside and invite Jon to church one more time. "This time," he reasons with himself, "I have the invitation card to help. I can just give Jon the card. Tell him about the new series that is starting and then leave. Three minutes, tops. I can do it."

Sam says a little prayer, gets up—invitation card in hand—and walks next door to Jon's office.

"Hey Jon," Sam says as he taps on Jon's open door.

"Oh, Sam. How are you?" Jon answers.

"I'm okay. I mean, it's a little crazy with what's been going on around here lately. But I'm doing well," says Sam.

Sam sees Jon glance toward the clock on his desk.

"Hey, I just wanted to invite you to the new series my church is starting this weekend," Sam says as he approaches Jon's desk and hands him the postcard. "It's about God's view on money. Thought you might find it interesting, considering . . ."

"Oh," Jon pauses and looks at the card, "you know, I saw an ad in the paper about this last weekend."

Sam says an immediate and silent word of thanks as a wave of relief washes over him. God is working in this! He knew it!

"Sounds, uh, interesting enough," Jon continues.

"Well, I'll be there on Sunday, at the 11:30 service. I'd love for you and Liz to join me," Sam says with a new sense of boldness. "There's a great program for your kids too."

"Um . . . let me talk to Liz. I don't know . . . Uh, no," Jon stammers. "Actually, you know what? Yeah. We can do that. We'll come to that 11:30 service."

"Great! The address and all of the details are on the back of the card. So I'll see you guys then," Jon says, trying to contain his excitement.

"Uh-huh. Yep. Sunday . . ." Jon murmurs. He's still looking at the postcard as Sam leaves his office.

Promotion, Preparation, and Planning

Not only do you need to plan and prepare for the guests who are going to come your way as a result of personal evangelism and promotion, but you also have to plan and prepare your promotion itself. If you want to create seeds that are going to be valuable and have an impact on the people you are trying to reach, you have to have a plan in place for molding your promotion into its most effective form. People like Jon will not connect with your newspaper ads, your invitation cards, or any of your other efforts unless you keep these five things in mind as you create them:

1. **Be consistent**—Make sure that your marketing efforts are not sporadic. People respond to consistency. For example, if you do a large-scale direct mail campaign in early February for your upcoming big day, do it every February. If you advertise in the local new resident packet, advertise every time a new packet comes out. Consistency is key.
2. **Be clear**—People say no to propositions that aren't clear to them, so your advertising needs to be unmistakably, crystal clear. Check and recheck your level of clarity. About 70 to 80 percent of the promotion that I see from churches

around the country is unclear. Sometimes I'm not even sure that what's being promoted is actually a church. Other times the material doesn't give me the information I need. And most often, they don't tell me what they want me to do. You have to be clear about what you are promoting and what you are asking people to do. No matter what form your promotion takes, it should always be an obvious invitation to come to your church.

I know a pastor who, in his excitement over the decision to put a billboard up in his community, let clarity fall to the curb. He created a beautiful billboard with a clever theme but failed to include his church's location. Now, this pastor is a smart guy and detail oriented, in general. But he fell into the common trap of getting caught up in a big promotion and overlooking the most obvious details. Make sure you include your church's name, where you meet, and the service time on every piece of promotion you create. Be clear that you are a church and that you want people to join you. Allow no room for confusion. Small clarifications make all the difference in the success of a promotional campaign. Remember, God is working in the lives of the people you will touch with this seed. Make every effort to ensure that the path to his truth is clear.

3. **Be creative**—Creativity is wonderful, as long as it is never at clarity's expense. Many churches make the mistake of being cute and clever over being clear, which leads to nothing but frustration for everyone involved. So be creative. Try something that no one else has ever tried. Just keep your creativity in line behind your clarity.

Church Leader Testimony

Our media team made a commercial that we put up on our website, on YouTube.com, and on MySpace.com. Being that I am also a national hip-hop artist, we themed the message around my new single entitled "Home," which was about coming back to God. We broke our highest attendance record, with over seven hundred people, and over seventy people built a relationship with Christ.

Tommy Kyllonen (aka Urban D), Pastor
Crossover Church (Tampa, FL)

4. **Be confined**—In advertising, as in life, you can't be all things to all people—and you shouldn't try to be. Allow the group you are targeting to confine the substance of your message. For example, if you are buying an ad in a wedding magazine, focus that promotion on what you have to offer newlyweds and other young couples. Don't clutter the space with information about your children's ministry. The majority of the target audience for your ad isn't to that life stage yet, so there's no reason to throw more information at them than they need. Avoid clutter, again, in the name of clarity.

5. **Be confident**—Your marketing is going to be out in the community facing competition from hundreds of secular marketing campaigns—and you have the advantage. Why? Because you have the Spirit of God working in and through your promotion. You can be confident that your efforts are going to reap a reward because they are being infused by God. Long before your ad campaign was ever conceived, God was working in the hearts of those people whose lives it would intersect. So be confident in the effort you are

making. Expect God to use your promotion to influence your community in ways you can't even imagine.

As you begin thinking about promoting your church in the community, don't neglect the power of prayer. Cover every aspect of your promotion. Pray for clarity as you design and prepare. Pray for God's blessing on each piece of promotion that goes out your door. Pray for the people whose lives are going to be intersected. I have literally laid hands on some of our biggest promotional mailings before they hit the post office—and for a guy who is ordained as a Baptist, that's saying a lot! The point is to make sure that you are asking God to do his will through these evangelism efforts and to bless the outreach for his glory. When you invite God into the details of your promotion, you'll be surprised at the consistency, clarity, creativity, and confidence he will give you.

Depending on the size of your city or town, you have thousands—maybe hundreds of thousands—of people all around you who are waiting for you to point them in the direction of truth. As you step out in faith, sow seed, and prepare for the harvest, you will begin to see amazing things happen in your church. Your congregation will get excited about reaching people. The evangelistic temperature of your church will hit the boiling point and start bubbling over as first-time guests begin coming to your church in record numbers.

God has called us to be wise farmers toiling in the fields so that he can work in cooperation with us to bring the harvest. Take a minute to wrap your mind around that reality. What a privilege we have to work with God in revealing himself to people who don't yet know him. But we have to be willing to do what is asked of us. So pinpoint your best fields, plant the maximum number of seeds possible, expect a proportional return, wait for the coming harvest, and while you are waiting, prepare and plan for the future. As you do, you will be clearing the way for every unchurched person in your community to say yes to God.

preservation

12

preparing the way

Helping People Take the Next Step

If you confess with your mouth that Jesus is Lord and believe in your heart that God raised him from the dead, you will be saved.

Romans 10:9

God hath given to man a short time here upon earth, and yet upon this short time eternity depends.

Jeremy Taylor

Now that we've explored the importance of the pastor's role in evangelism, thought through the true potential of personal outreach, and discovered the power of promotion, let's step back and reexamine the ultimate purpose of this journey we've taken together. As I said early on, the evangelism system begins when an unchurched person is prompted by the Spirit to attend your church and ends when that person follows Jesus Christ, is baptized, and is moving toward church membership. Before your new person can be baptized, he has to say yes to Jesus. That yes is the goal of all of your evangelistic efforts. Your harvest is born through the accumulation of each and every affirmation. So once you sow the seeds of evangelism, you have to know how to preserve the crop—or how to help each person God brings you to say yes to the gospel of Jesus Christ.

Most people have to baby-step their way into big decisions. Thanks once again to human nature, we have a self-protection mechanism that causes us to approach life-changing circumstances slowly. We don't get married after a first date. We don't move to a new city without a lot of deliberation. We don't accept a job without knowing what will be expected of us. We get the facts and we take small steps. We get to know our future spouse over a number of years; we line up an apartment and make connections; we talk to our potential boss and study the job requirements. These baby steps make us comfortable enough to take the plunge.

Of course, things work a little differently when the Holy Spirit is involved. He can cause us to take major leaps of faith without much human understanding. But for the majority of unchurched individuals, there is still a baby-step process involved in being ready to accept Jesus's offer of salvation. Once we have moved unbelievers out of the community and into our crowd, we can help them take those baby steps a little more confidently. First we have to invite them, as often and as clearly as possible, to say yes to Jesus. Then we must do our part to help them answer in the affirmative.

Inviting People to Say Yes

The single best way to encourage unbelievers to say yes to Jesus is to invite them to. Never miss a chance to call for a commitment. You have the opportunity to invite people into a relationship with God at all levels of your ministry. The Sunday service is an ideal time to urge your attenders to make an immediate decision. Tell them not to wait. God may be knocking loudly on their hearts; push them to open the door right away. Make sure you are also encouraging people to say yes to God through your small groups and in membership classes. Being a Christian should be one of the requirements for new members, so take time in every membership class to call for a commitment.

Try building baby steps into your Sunday services to help those who aren't quite ready to step over the line. Often I will call for a commitment to Christ and also provide a "next step" for those who aren't sure. I will encourage my attenders who are wrestling with God to learn more about what it means to be a Christian. To help them get started, I offer a "What Does It Mean to Be a Christian?" DVD every week at our resource table, and I let them know that the DVD will walk them through a clear presentation of the gospel. (Visit www.ignitebook.com for a copy of the "What Does It Mean to Be a Christian?" DVD.) I also ask them to let me know, by marking it on their Connection Card, if they are considering giving their life to Christ. If they take that step, I will send them some information or perhaps give them a call. My goal is to help them take small steps that will ultimately make them comfortable enough to say yes to the Spirit's drawing.

One of the most effective baby-step tools we've used at The Journey is our "Annual Spiritual Survey." At the end of our Easter services each year, I ask everyone in attendance to participate in a live survey with me—a survey that has already been set up on the back of their Connection Card. I have them look at the back of their card, where they find the letters A, B, C, and D printed. Then I say something like this:

> Today I want to do a spiritual survey to see where people in our congregation stand in their relationship with Christ. If you are a believer, would you circle the letter A? That will be most of you. If you are asking Jesus to come into your life for the first time today, would you let me know that by circling the letter B? I would like to follow up with you and send you some materials to help you get started in your new Christian faith. If you are considering turning your life over to God but aren't quite ready to make that decision, would you circle the letter C? Or if you are here today but you don't believe what we've been talking about and you don't think you'll ever believe, would you be candid enough to let me know that by circling the letter D?

Asking people to honestly evaluate their spiritual standing gets them thinking, which often causes them to open their hearts enough for the Holy Spirit to start working. After years of doing this survey, I have seen an interesting trend. Almost every person who circles the letter D becomes a Christian in our church within the year. I've seen it happen almost without exception. Admitting that you don't believe in God and claiming that you never will is an affront to him. Inevitably, God begins working in the lives of those people so intensely that they end up coming to the point of salvation. I love having someone approach me in membership class or after a baptism and say, "You know, last Easter I took that spiritual survey and circled the D." Amazingly, it happens all the time.

God is continually drawing people to himself. He uses as many different circumstances and scenarios as there are people to draw. I encourage you to think back to your own story of salvation. How did God first speak to you? Do you remember how you thought before you knew God? Sometimes we get so used to being Christians that we forget the power of our own cleansing. The more we reflect on how God brought us into his kingdom, the better we will be at helping others find the door.

To that same end, we should always be encouraging our regular attenders and members to think about their own testimony. I like to challenge them to write it out using this form:

My Testimony Worksheet (Based on Acts 26)

My Life Before Becoming a Christian:

_____

_____

_____

_____

How I Became a Christian:

_____

_____

_____

_____

My Life After Becoming a Christian:

_____

_____

_____

_____

Writing out their testimony helps them put the story of how God changed their life into words. They will then be better able to articulate their testimony to friends and acquaintances, when God gives them the opportunity to witness. If you've never completed a form like this yourself, I challenge you to take a few minutes to do so. Making an intentional effort to focus on your God-story will help you relate to and connect with those you are asking to say yes to the gospel.

My salvation story is an interesting one: I became a follower of Jesus a little differently, and a little later, than most people might expect. I actually asked Jesus to come into my life right around my eighteenth birthday. Until that point, I had been consumed with some other things. I started a computer business while I was in high school. When I hit seventeen, I was working on an engineering degree at North Carolina State University while traveling and speaking at different conferences for young entrepreneurs. At one of these conferences, I met a guy who had written a book I wanted to read, so I headed to a local bookstore to pick it up. While I was there, I noticed a book by Billy Graham called *Peace with God*. I bought Dr. Graham's book on a whim, thinking it was a history book about a guy I had heard a little about while growing up in North Carolina.

In October of 1989, I was reading through *Peace with God* and got to the page where Billy Graham offered an invitation of salvation to anyone reading the book who didn't know Jesus. I prayed the prayer that he had typed out for me there and then saw a toll-free number that he suggested I call. I went back to my little apartment in Raleigh and called the 800 number. Yep, I'm that guy. The person on the other end suggested I do a few things: read my Bible, pray, get involved in a good church, and make my decision public through baptism.

After I gave my life to God, he put me on an entirely new path. I ended up getting my bachelor's degree in religion and psychology at Gardner-Webb University and then a master of divinity degree at Duke University while pastoring a little church outside of Charlotte. Eventually I moved to Southern California to work with Rick Warren and Saddleback Church. Then, in 2000, my wife Kelley and I moved to Manhattan to start The Journey.

Obviously, I was invited to say yes to God in a relatively unique way, which underscores an important truth—God is at work. As pastors and church leaders, you and I have to do our part to direct people toward his gospel and clearly show them what to do with it. Billy Graham invited me to say yes to God through a book. I invite people to say yes to God through Sunday services, small groups, membership classes, and personal conversations. As we follow through on our calling and make the invitation, God will prompt people to accept it. For those who aren't ready, you can urge them down the path by encouraging them to take baby steps. Make sure you are continually extending the invitation. To get people into our churches and then not invite them to say yes to Jesus would be a horrible disservice to them and to God.

Preparing for People to Say Yes

In addition to inviting people to say yes to God, we have to prepare for them to say yes. God will not draw people to himself in your church unless you are prepared. This goes back to the principle of spiritual readiness that we explored in the last chapter. Why would

God cause people to accept his invitation of salvation under your care if you aren't ready to receive them and start shepherding them toward becoming fully developing followers of Jesus? Preparing for people to say yes to God is more an assimilation discussion than an evangelism one. The process of clearing the way for them to meet God in a personal way begins the minute they decide to visit your church for the first time. The assimilation system that I detail in *Fusion: Turning First-Time Guests into Fully-Engaged Members of Your Church* outlines the process for making sure a first-time attender comes back again and again until they are ready to accept Jesus's invitation of salvation, join your church, and become fully developing followers of Christ.

The assimilation system begins to overlap the evangelism system when your evangelistic efforts result in that first-time guest showing up at your door. I highly recommend that you commit to studying and implementing a strong assimilation system in the same way that you have committed to taking your evangelism to a new level. God causes the two to work together as he works through them to bring new people into the kingdom. In fact, while we are touching on the topic of assimilation, let me fast-forward our friend Jon's story. You will have to read *Fusion* to see how Jon and Liz's first visit to FCC went and how they eventually come to the point of attending this membership class.

As Tim finishes outlining the vision for FCC's future outreach, Jon and Liz exchange impressed glances. Still, Jon can't shake an uneasy feeling that something is not quite right with all of this. Over the last few weeks, he has heard Tim and the other pastors talk about a personal relationship with God, but

Jon has always forced himself to tune out. That's the part that doesn't quite make sense to him—or does it?

"Now let's talk about the requirements for membership here at FCC," Tim says from the front of the room. "The first and most important requirement is that you are a Christian—that you have come to a point in your life where you have acknowledged your need for Christ and accepted him as your personal Savior. In Romans, Paul tells us that . . ."

As Tim continues to speak, Jon finds himself listening more intently than ever before. For some strange reason, he feels as if Tim is speaking directly to him. His hands start to sweat a little. He looks over at Liz to see if she is feeling this too. Her eyes are locked on Tim.

"If there is anyone in this class today who has not yet accepted Christ, I want to invite you to do so right now. You wouldn't be sitting here, seeking out information on joining this church, if Jesus had not been calling you to himself. Before you take the step to become a member of his family, you must say yes to him on a personal level. If I am talking to you, bow your head and pray this prayer with me . . ."

Jon bows his head and squints his eyes closed, his heart thumping loudly in his ears. Every word that Tim prays, Jon repeats emphatically to himself. Liz's hand finds his with a squeeze. He intertwines his fingers with hers, lets out a deep breath, and continues to pray.

Pastor Tim used FCC's membership class as an opportunity to call his new attenders into a relationship with Jesus. But well before he invited anyone to say yes to God, he had been preparing

153

the way for them to say yes. He knew that many of the attenders in that membership class did not yet have a personal relationship with Jesus. Part of preparing for people to say yes to God, on the evangelistic side of things, is making sure you know where the people in your church stand. How? By developing a tracking system that will keep you on top of who has said yes to Jesus and who has not. People should be letting you know when they make a decision for Christ, either by marking it on the back of a Connection Card or by coming to see you personally. The tracking system you use is a matter of your church's culture and your personal choice. Just make sure that people know how to let you know when they say yes to God, in whatever form you establish.

Church Leader Testimony

We launched a prayer campaign called "6,000 minutes of prayer," in which we challenged one hundred people to commit to twenty minutes of prayer for the three weeks preceding Easter weekend. To maximize our opportunities to invite new guests, we challenged our people to make a goal of inviting ten new guests. We also offered one hundred families free lunch cards to a local favorite restaurant so they could take their guests to lunch following the service. In the end, we had a record attendance for our church, and forty-one people made a decision to accept Jesus.

Joel Eason, Senior Pastor
Bridgeway Church (Tampa, FL)

Following Up When People Say Yes

When an unbeliever makes the decision to give his life to Christ in your church, your next step is to follow up with him right away. This new Christian may or may not have a grasp on what the decision he just made really means. He has no idea what to do next. That's why God has positioned you in his life. Thankfully, you are prepared with a plan and with tools to help him begin his Christian walk.

At The Journey, the first thing I want a brand-new believer to do is indicate his decision to follow Christ on the back of his Connection Card. That way, I will know about his decision as soon as the cards are gathered and processed on Monday. Once I have all of the names and email addresses of those who made a first-time commitment, I send a personal email to congratulate them on deciding to follow Jesus. I make sure that the email is in their in-box the Monday after their decision. The email includes a link to an online Bible study. (See appendix 6 for a copy of my new believer email and letter or visit www. ignitebook.com to download a copy.)

During the first week of their new life with Christ, each new believer will get some follow-up material from me in the mail. I include the book *The Next Step for Your Journey* (a book I wrote for new believers), plus some information about our church and about baptism. Baptism is their next step, and I want to ensure that they take the step within a month or two. When dealing with a new believer, focus on getting their questions answered and getting them connected. Make sure the forward momentum continues and no one falls through the cracks. If someone lets you know that they accepted Christ at your church and then you don't hear from them or see them for a month, there's a problem. You need to pick up the telephone and see what is going on. (You can download a PDF of *The Next Step for Your Journey* at www.ignitebook.com.)

Following Up with New Believers

Following up on new believers is a very important task for any pastor. Our faithfulness with the few will prove our trustworthiness with the many. (Hey, that sounds like something Jesus said one time!) While each church must wrestle with their own new believer process, the goal is to be clear and intentional. Ask these questions:

- **What do you want a new believer to do in the first hour after becoming a follower of Jesus?** At The Journey, we invite them to check the box on their Connection Card. Other churches invite them to come forward during an invitation time. I'm not against come-forward invitations. If you use them, just make sure you also have a way for those who are so introverted that they will never come forward to register a decision within the first hour.
- **What do you want a new believer to receive within one day of becoming a follower of Jesus?** For us, it's the email you can find in appendix 6, with a link to an online Bible study.
- **What do you want a new believer to do within one week of becoming a follower of Jesus?** We want to put a new believer's book in their hand to help them start growing in their faith.
- **What steps do we want a new believer to take in the first month?** At The Journey, the answer is baptism.
- **What's the future plan of discipleship for a new believer?** For us, it's connecting them into a small group and normalizing their church attendance.

There's no such thing as a perfect new believer process—remember that the birds, sun, thorns, and weeds are working against you—but do everything you can to ensure that the new "babe in Christ" whom God has entrusted to you has the best chance to grow!

These new believers are the harvest God has given you out of the seeds you worked so hard to sow. Put a system in place to follow up with them. Otherwise, your ignited evangelism will turn to ashes and smoke at the critical juncture. Return the crop to God by making sure that no one gets left behind—and by celebrating the newest members of the ever-growing family of God.

13

the celebration

Let the Fun Begin!

But his father said to the servants, "Quick! Bring the finest robe in the house and put it on him. Get a ring for his finger and sandals for his feet. And kill the calf we have been fattening. We must celebrate with a feast, for this son of mine was dead and has now returned to life. He was lost, but now he is found." So the party began.

Luke 15:22–24

I think we all sin by needlessly disobeying the apostolic injunction to "rejoice" as much as by anything else.

C. S. Lewis

As the crowd settles into the rows of seats, Pastor Tim taps the microphone with his finger and says, "Good afternoon, everyone! Let me take a minute to thank each and every one of you for coming out for today's baptism celebration!"

Cheers and applause erupt from the audience.

"If you have been around FCC for long, you understand the significance of what we are doing here today—and by your cheers, I can tell that most of you do! You are about to meet over forty people who have given their lives to Jesus and who, in just a few minutes, are going to make that decision public by following the command to be baptized. If you are here because you have a friend or family member being baptized, we are so glad you joined us for this celebration!"

As Tim is speaking, Jon glances into the seated crowd from his position by the wall. He sees Sam sitting in the second row. As if on cue, Sam turns and catches his eye. He is beaming. Jon smiles back and grabs Liz's hand.

Liz scans the crowd, looking for her mom and the kids. She's a little nervous because her mom hasn't been to church in over fifteen years. The biggest reason she agreed to come today is because Liz asked her to bring the kids. Secretly, Liz is hoping that the baptism celebration will stir something in her mom's heart and get her interested in seeking God—for real, this time.

"As we baptize each of the new believers you see here before you today," Tim says as he motions toward the waiting line along the wall, "we are signifying an important transformation. When they step into the water, they represent their old life, apart from Jesus. When I immerse them underneath the water, that represents the cleansing that took place when they accepted Jesus's invitation of salvation. As I lift them out of the water, they are being raised to walk in newness of life—in the resurrected life of Jesus Christ. Let's get started . . ."

Jon and Liz wait patiently as Tim and a couple of the other pastors baptize those in front of them. When it's their turn, they enter the water together.

"Jon and Liz," Tim says, "have you both accepted Jesus Christ as your Lord and Savior?"

They both nod the affirmative.

"Then," Tim continues, "by your profession of faith, I baptize you in the name of the Father, the Son, and the Holy Ghost." Tim and his associate pastor baptize Jon and Liz. As they go under with linked arms, they hear Tim say, "Buried with Jesus in death." Then, as they are lifted back up, "And raised to walk in newness of life."

At that, the crowd erupts with whoops and applause. Jon and Liz's many new friends stand and cheer as the two wipe water from their eyes and embrace.

Before they are able to leave the baptistery, Tim says, "Just one second, guys. I want to do something special here. Sam, could you join me up front?"

Sam, looking surprised, gets out of his seat and walks to the baptistery.

"I just want to tell you all a brief story," says Tim. "Several months ago, Sam confided in me about a guy in his office whom he had been inviting to church."

Sam glances at Jon and lets out a little laugh.

Tim continues, "He had asked this guy to come to church with him several times, but it wasn't working out."

Jon gives an embarrassed shrug.

"I encouraged Sam to keep asking, because this guy—yep, you guessed it, Jon here—was really on his heart. So when our big Financial Peace series rolled around, Sam asked Jon to come to church with him one more time and gave him a postcard for the series. Well, as you can see, Jon accepted! And here he and his wife Liz are today, rejoicing in their new life in Christ!"

A dripping wet Jon walks over and bear-hugs Sam, making the crowd laugh.

"This is what it's all about," Pastor Tim says. "Making disciples. Great job, Sam. Congratulations, Jon and Liz. We are so happy for you."

The applause continues as Jon, Liz, and Sam leave the baptistery. Liz looks into the crowd again and spots Madison waving at her. Liz gives a little wave back, and as she does she sees her mother wiping a tear from her eye.

Baptism is a reason to celebrate! Not only does it signal a new fully developing follower of Jesus, it is also the culmination of your evangelism system. With every new person you baptize, you are witnessing God working through your evangelism system in a powerful way. You encouraged evangelism through the stage; you asked people to pray for and invite their friends to church; you kept the evangelistic temperature of your church hot; you gave your people tools for sharing with those in their lives; you made your church known in the community; God worked through your sowing to bring you the unchurched; you were prepared and you invited them to say yes to him; and he drew them into accepting his Son as their Lord under your care. What's not to celebrate? You get to be a part of the incredible plan that God is unfolding in your community.

If the process you witness as an unchurched person becomes a believer and gets baptized isn't enough reason to celebrate, let's add this: celebrating when people come to God is biblical. Take a minute to read through Jesus's words in Luke 15:4–7:

> If a man has a hundred sheep and one of them gets lost, what will he do? Won't he leave the ninety-nine others in the wilderness and go to search for the one that is lost until he finds it? And when he has found it, he will joyfully carry it home on his shoulders. When he arrives, he will call together his friends and neighbors, saying, "Rejoice with me because I have found my lost sheep." In the same way, there is more joy in heaven over one lost sinner who repents and returns to God than over ninety-nine others who are righteous and haven't strayed away!

If there's joy in heaven when one sinner returns to God, there should be joy on earth too. Take a look at Luke 15:8–9:

> Or suppose a woman has ten silver coins and loses one. Won't she light a lamp and sweep the entire house and search carefully until she finds it? And when she finds it, she will call in her friends and neighbors and say, "Rejoice with me because I have found my lost coin."

Again, we are called to rejoice. Jesus feels so strongly about celebrating when an unchurched person comes to know him that he goes on to illustrate the point a third way, through the story of the prodigal son. He really doesn't want us to miss this. Take a look at Luke 15:20–24, just after the prodigal decides to return home to his father:

> So he returned home to his father. And while he was still a long way off, his father saw him coming. Filled with love and compassion, he ran to his son, embraced him, and kissed him. His son

said to him, "Father, I have sinned against both heaven and you, and I am no longer worthy of being called your son." But his father said to the servants, "Quick! Bring the finest robe in the house and put it on him. Get a ring for his finger and sandals for his feet. And kill the calf we have been fattening. We must celebrate with a feast, for this son of mine was dead and has now returned to life. He was lost, but now he is found." So the party began.

Each of Jesus's three parables ends with a call to celebrate. Whenever you have a chance to celebrate any kind of evangelistic efforts, do it. Here are three particularly effective ways to celebrate evangelistic success with your people:

- **Tell stories.** Let people know that evangelism is continually happening in your church. For example, when someone who first came to you through a servant evangelism outreach is baptized or takes the step of membership, make people aware. Have that person tell her story. Your members and regular attenders will get more fired up about reaching out to the community.

  Or when someone brings a friend to church who goes on to say yes to God and get baptized, let the new person tell his story. Tell stories from the stage about people you have personally reached out to. Tell stories you hear from within your church about people who are passionate about personal evangelism. Stories touch the hearts of your people and keep the congregation excited about evangelism.
- **Share statistics and numbers.** If you really push your people to invite their friends to church for the few weeks before a big day and then you have a great turnout, celebrate those

164

numbers. Send an email to your members letting them know what your attendance was and how many first-time guests you had. Celebrate the fruit of the personal evangelism you had been encouraging.

In the same way, keep track of your numbers every month throughout the year. If you do a lot of outreach over the summer and then have a particularly large fall, share those stats. Let people know that their willingness to get involved in outreach pays off. At the end of every six-month or one-year period, celebrate the number of new believers in your church. If you keep numbers and statistics in front of your people, in the right spirit, you will help them stay outwardly focused.

- **Congratulate people who bring their friends to church.** Send them a handwritten note and include a little gift, as I mentioned earlier. Take Pastor Tim's lead and introduce the Sams of your church at your baptism celebrations. From time to time, throw out an extra incentive, like a free book, for people who bring their friends to church the next week— and then put a letter of thanks in the books you hand out. Just let people know that you appreciate their efforts to reach their friends for Jesus. Your positive reinforcement and encouragement will keep them reaching out.

Celebrating your harvest will honor God, excite people, and keep your evangelism system ignited. Every time you tell a story, share a stat, or congratulate someone, you have an opportunity to do two things. One, you can cast your vision for evangelism anew. Two, you are able to publicly give God the glory for blessing your church.

As we've seen, going after that lost sheep, that lost coin, and that straying son requires some refocusing. The danger we all run into is paying so much attention to the ninety-nine sheep with us that we don't have time to think about that one that's lost out in the wilderness. But we don't get to set our priorities for ministry—God is in charge of that. And according to his Word, God would have us go out and find that lost sheep. Sometimes that means reprioritizing. Sometimes that means putting a few of your plans for the rest of the flock on hold.

Create an atmosphere within your church where people care about the community outside your doors. As you now know, this starts with the senior pastor and the staff. You may have to rework your budget with your new evangelism goals in mind. You may need to redistribute some of your ministry time. Do whatever you need to do to obey Jesus's command to "Go and make disciples of all the nations, baptizing them in the name of the Father and the Son and the Holy Spirit" (Matt. 28:19). Have you ever really thought about Jesus's words at the end of the Great Commission? "And be sure of this," he says, "I am with you always, even to the end of the age" (Matt. 28:20). God is with you in the work of reaching unbelievers. If God is for you, who can be against you?

conclusion

Keep On Dreaming

The master was full of praise. "Well done, my good and faithful servant. You have been faithful in handling this small amount, so now I will give you many more responsibilities. Let's celebrate together!"

Matthew 25:21

Some wish to live within the sound of a chapel bell; I wish to run a rescue mission within a yard of hell.

C. T. Studd

At the beginning of this book, I asked you to dream with me. Remember? I asked you to consider "What if your church could double in a day?" What did that question rouse in you? Doubt? Fear? Indignation? Now, having studied the evangelism system put forth in these pages, let me ask you to dream with me again: what if your church really could double in a day? How do you feel about that question now? Think about

167

this one: what if, over the next twelve months, more people came to Christ than ever before in your church's history? What if the number of attenders you have now becomes the number of people you baptize five years from now?

Think of the rejoicing that would happen in heaven if you allowed yourself to think deeply about these questions and then follow through and go to work to make them a reality, in the power of the Spirit. God has big dreams for your church. Bigger than you can imagine. And he has called you to do the work. He is calling you to sow the seeds. As you do, he will add his Spirit to them. My prayer for you is that you will latch on to and implement the process I've detailed here. Make the changes that need to be made in your church. Mobilize your people for evangelism. Keep the evangelistic temperature boiling hot. And then give God the praise as he sends you the harvest.

Galatians 6:9 encourages, "Let's not get tired of doing what is good. At just the right time we will reap a harvest of blessing if we don't give up." God will send you the harvest of blessing if you don't tire of doing what is good when the suffering comes. His Word says so. God cannot be mocked. If you sincerely ask him to guide and ignite your passion and plan for evangelism and then you commit yourself to doing your part of the work, the next day of Pentecost may just be in your church.

It's Friday afternoon. Jon sits at his desk, staring at the FCC invitation card he brought to work with him. He's nervous. In the past, he has swallowed the nerves that tried to keep him from inviting Kevin to church, but he's beginning to get embarrassed. He has already asked Kevin twice and Kevin said no both times

. . . something about being busy. Still, Jon can't shake the sense that he needs to put his own feelings and fears aside and invite Kevin to church one more time, just like Sam did for him. Jon says a little prayer, gets up—invitation card in hand—and walks next door to Kevin's office. . . .

postscript

I hope this book will become a conversation starter between us. I am constantly developing resources and gathering ideas from others to help you cooperate with God to see as many unchurched people as possible follow Jesus in baptism and move toward membership in your church. I would love to hear your story and discuss ways we can grow together for God's glory. Please contact me through this book's website: www.ignitebook.com.

Your partner in ministry,

Nelson Searcy
Lead Pastor, The Journey Church, www.journeymetro.com
Founder, www.churchleaderinsights.com

appendix 1

baptism

Explaining Baptism

Here's a sample of information we provide to baptism candidates at The Journey.

What Is the Meaning of Baptism?

Baptism illustrates Christ's burial and resurrection.

Christ died for our sins . . . He was buried, and . . . He rose again.

1 Corinthians 15:3–4 NKJV

For when you were baptized, you were buried with Christ, and in baptism you were also raised with Christ.

Colossians 2:12 GNT

Baptism illustrates your new life as a Christian.

What this means is that those who become Christians become new persons. They are not the same anymore, for the old life is gone. A new life has begun!

2 Corinthians 5:17 NLT

By our baptism then, we were buried with Him and shared His death, in order that, just as Christ was raised from the dead . . . so also we may live a new life!

Romans 6:4 GNT

Baptism doesn't make you a believer—it shows that you already believe. Baptism does not "save" you; only your faith in Christ does that. Baptism is like a wedding ring; it's the outward symbol of the commitment you make in your heart.

For it is by grace you have been saved, through faith . . . it is the gift of God—not by works, so that no one can boast.

Ephesians 2:8–9 NIV

Why Be Baptized by Immersion?

Jesus was baptized that way.

As soon as Jesus was baptized, he went up out of the water.

Matthew 3:16 NIV

Every baptism in the Bible was by immersion. For example:

Then both Philip and the eunuch went down into the water and Philip baptized him. *When they came up out of the water*, the Spirit of the Lord suddenly took Philip away.

Acts 8:38–39 NIV, emphasis added

The Greek word *baptize* means "to immerse or dip under water." It best symbolized a burial and resurrection!

The founders of denominations agree:

I would have those who are to be baptized to be entirely immersed, as the work imports and the mystery signifies.

Martin Luther

The word "baptize" signifies to immerse. It is certain that immersion was the practice of the ancient church.

John Calvin

Buried with Him, alludes to baptizing by immersion according to the custom of the first church.

John Wesley

Who Should Be Baptized?

Every person who has believed in Christ.

Those who believed what Peter said were baptized and added to the church.

Acts 2:41 NLT

But when they believed Philip as he preached the good news
. . . and the name of Jesus Christ, they were baptized, both
men and women.

Acts 8:12 NIV

Simon himself believed and was baptized.

Acts 8:13

At The Journey, we wait until children are old enough to
believe and to understand the true meaning of baptism before
we baptize them.

Some churches practice a "baptism of confirmation" for children. This ceremony is intended to be a covenant between the
parents and God on the behalf of the child. The parents promise
to raise their child in the faith until the child is old enough to
make their own personal confession of Christ. This custom began
about three hundred years after the Bible was completed.

This is different from the baptism talked about in the Bible,
which was only for those old enough to believe. The purpose is
to publicly confess your personal commitment to Christ.

When Should I Be Baptized?

As soon as you have believed.

Those who believed . . . were baptized . . . that day.

Acts 2:41

Then Philip began with that very passage of Scripture and told
him the good news about Jesus.

As they traveled along the road, they came to some water
and the eunuch said, "Look, here is water. Why shouldn't I be

baptized?" And he gave orders to stop the chariot. Then both Philip and the eunuch went down into the water and Philip baptized him.

Acts 8:35–38 NIV

There is no reason to delay. As soon as you have decided to receive Christ into your life, you can and should be baptized. If you wait until you are "perfect," you'll never feel good enough!

Can My Family and Friends Be Baptized Together?

Yes! If each person understands fully the meaning of baptism, and each one has personally placed his or her trust in Christ for salvation, we encourage families to be baptized at the same time. It is a wonderful expression of commitment.

However, it is important to remember that baptism is a personal statement of faith, not a family or group tradition. It is usually not wise to delay your baptism while waiting for others to join you. This puts an undue pressure on them and delays your obedience.

What Should I Wear When I Am Baptized?

Women should wear shorts and a top or a swimsuit. Men may wear shorts, T-shirts, or a swimsuit. Bring a change of clothes, a towel, and a plastic bag for your wet clothes.

Will I Have to Say Anything?

At the beginning of the service, Pastor Nelson will briefly explain the meaning of baptism. You will wait in the water for your turn to be baptized. The pastor will introduce you, briefly lower you just under the water, and then you can leave the water, dry off, and watch the others. Later you will receive your baptism certificate. We encourage you to invite all your relatives and friends to attend your baptism.

What Happens After Baptism?

Baptism is a very important event in the life of any new Christian. I know that as pastors we all go to great lengths to make sure the celebration is done just right. But what about the day or week after the baptism service? What's your follow-up plan?

I've noticed that the week after a person's baptism can be a trying time. Here are a few thoughts on why:

- Satan isn't happy.
- Their friends and family have a lot of tough questions.
- They personally have a lot of doubts ("Am I really saved?" "Am I worthy?").
- An external trial (i.e., an argument at work or with a spouse) takes on a higher level of meaning because the baptism was so recent.

Here's my process for following up on those who are baptized:

- We pray for all baptism candidates at the Sunday service. I ask our congregation to pray for them throughout the week too.
- As a staff we divide up the names and pray for each person throughout the week.

Post-Baptism Email (Sent with a Baptism Picture)

From: Nelson Searcy

Subject: Congratulations on your baptism!

Attachment: Baptism picture

Dear _____,

I want to congratulate you on taking this step to be baptized! Baptism is a first and extremely important step of obedience as you walk with Jesus Christ. In Romans 6:4 Paul describes baptism like this: "For we died and were buried with Christ by baptism. And just as Christ was raised from the dead by the glorious power of the Father, now we also may live new lives."

When you face times of difficulty and doubt in the future, look back to the day of your baptism. Remember that on July 26, 2008, you publicly proclaimed that you were going to follow Jesus for the rest of your life. I will pray for you as you continue to take steps each day to trust in Christ and live this new life in the power of his resurrection. Some of the very important steps you can take are:

1. Daily prayer and Bible reading. In fact, this Sunday we will be talking about the habit of Bible study in our new series entitled "Accelerate." Here's a link to a website that offers several options for reading through the Bible; just select the one that best fits your lifestyle: http://biblestudytools.com/bibleinayear
2. Share your faith with your friends. Invite your friends to come to church with you, stop by the resource table in the back, and give them a free copy of the CD "What Does It Mean to Be a Christian?"

Please let me know if there is anything I can do for you.

Have a great week, and God bless!

Nelson

P.S.: Join us on Sunday as we kick off our new series "Accelerate: 5 Habits to Accelerate My Spiritual Growth." I'll see you there.

Nelson Searcy

Lead Pastor, The Journey

The Journey Church of the City

One Church: Three Locations: Six Services

www.journeymetro.com

- I email each person a copy of their baptism "group picture" and an encouraging note from me (see the email on p. 179).
- We mail each person a copy of his or her baptism certificate.
- We follow up with them in about a month to make sure they are signed up for a small group.

This isn't everything we do, but it's the highlights. The key point I want to make is that you need a follow-up process.

Even if you haven't had a lot of baptisms lately, sit down and think through your process. Write it out; discuss it with your leaders; ask God to give you wisdom! I heard someone say one time that "if you are faithful with the few, you will be given even more."

appendix 2

fasting

What is fasting?
• Abstaining from something, usually food, for spiritual purposes.

What does the Bible say about fasting?
• Biblical examples: Moses (see Exod. 34:28; Deut. 9:9, 18); David (see 2 Sam. 12:16); Nehemiah (see Neh. 1:4); Esther (Esther 4:16); Daniel (see Dan. 1:12); Anna (see Luke 2:37); Paul (see Acts 14:23); Jesus (see Matt. 4:1–2); the early church (see Acts 13:2).
• Jesus placed fasting on the same level as financial giving and prayer (see Matt. 6:1–18).
• Jesus said that there is a time for fasting (see Matt. 9:15).
• Paul says we should give ourselves at times to prayer and fasting (see 1 Cor. 7:5).

What is the purpose of fasting?
• The *primary purpose* of fasting is to focus on God and to center our attention on him. In doing so, we glorify God (see Zech. 7:5).

- Outer fasting is to lead to inner prayer, worship, and devotion. We "fast on food so we can feast on God."
- Fasting is not for personal glory or any other selfish motives (see Matt. 6:16–18).
- There are also some *secondary purposes* of fasting: fasting can reveal nonessential things that control us and take precedence in our lives (see 1 Cor. 6:12); fasting can increase the effectiveness of prayer (see 2 Sam. 12:16); fasting can bring guidance from God in decisions (see Acts 14:23); fasting can bring revelations (see Acts 13:2); fasting can help our physical well-being (Dan. 1:12); fasting can aid in concentration; fasting can help bring deliverance for those who are in bondage.
- But these benefits come only when fasting is our attempt to diligently seek God.

What are the different types of fasting?

- *Absolute fast*: no food or water for a period of time (see Exod. 34:28; Esther 4:16)
- *Normal fast*: only water, but no food or other drink
- *Partial fast*: usually only water, juices, and sometimes fruit (see Dan. 1:12)
- *Lenten fast*: giving up something specific for the duration of Lent (Ash Wednesday through Easter Sunday)
- *Fasting from other things*: people, media, telephone, certain activities/habits, etc.

appendix 3

invest and invite cards

The following is a list of 3 people I am attempting to invest in and invite to The Journey.

1. _____
2. _____
3. _____

I WILL
• Pray daily for them
• Share my own verbal witness.
• Invite them to The Journey.

Signature _____ Date _____ © www.nyjourney.com

Journey
Invest
and Invite
Card
"Live wisely among those who are not Christians, and make the most of every opportunity."
– Colossians 4:5

I will seek to invest in others who do not have a personal relationship with Jesus Christ and invite them to The Journey.

For the latest version of our Invest and Invite Card or to download this card, visit www.ignitebook.com.

appendix 4

what is servant evangelism?

Definition: Servant evangelism is sharing the love and message of Jesus Christ through simple acts of service and kindness. Servant evangelism is a biblical, fun, simple, and intentional way to make sharing Jesus a lifestyle!

Description: An individual or group begins doing intentional acts of kindness in their community with the aim of evangelism. Projects could include serving people by giving out free bottles of water on a hot day, passing out free granola bars to people on their way to work, or delivering gifts to local firemen or policemen. In addition to being served, each person is also given a card inviting them to church. On each card is information about the church, including service times, phone number, location, and any other information the church wishes to share.

Servant evangelism is a wonderful expression of the Great Commandment and the Great Commission. It is great for people who are first learning how to share their faith as well as for the most seasoned Christian!

appendix 5

how to conduct a Servant Evangelism Saturday

Servant Evangelism Defined

Servant evangelism (SE) is sharing the love and message of Jesus Christ through practical acts of service and kindness. Servant evangelism is a biblical, fun, simple, and intentional way to make sharing Jesus a lifestyle.

Servant Evangelism Described

Servant evangelism can be done individually or as a group. Here is the simple concept: an individual or group begins doing intentional acts of kindness in their community with the aim of evangelism. A simple act of kindness opens an unbeliever up to the greatest act of kindness of all: the gospel.

Servant evangelism involves two parts: service (i.e., acts of kindness) and evangelism. Many people in our culture today believe that the church is only concerned with getting something from them. By doing servant evangelism, the church is doing more than just being nice. It is breaking down one of the major barriers that keep people from experiencing the gospel.

Servant evangelism is a wonderful expression of the Great Commandment and the Great Commission. It is great for people who are first learning how to share their faith as well as for the most seasoned Christian.

Servant Evangelism Saturday Defined

A Journey-style Servant Evangelism Saturday is a one-Saturday-a-month event designed to engage attenders of the church in servant evangelism. The events are designed so that anyone can participate effectively—no prior training or preparation on the part of the participant is necessary.

Generic Project Calendar: Key Tasks

1. Select date for the project
2. Three weeks before your selected date:
   a. Design series-specific card about your church for use during the event
   b. Place date and brief information on your church calendar (don't forget your website calendar)
3. Two weeks before:
   a. Select project
   b. Select location
   c. Contact leaders of the groups that are signed up for the upcoming event
      i. Remind them about the event
      ii. Ask them to get a count of how many people from their group will be attending

    d. Provide some information in Sunday program on the upcoming event

    e. Print the series-specific card about your church

4. One week before:

    a. Flier in Sunday program on upcoming event

    b. Brief information in your weekly newsletter on the event

    c. Call group leaders and get the number from their group who will be attending

    d. Email group members directly and remind them about the event

    e. Purchase and prepare supplies and materials for the event

5. Post-event:

    a. Debrief on event with key leaders

    b. Begin developing plan for the next Servant Evangelism Saturday

The Journey System for Servant Evangelism Saturdays

1. Select the date for your next Servant Evangelism Saturday at least three weeks in advance.

At The Journey, we believe it is important to build as much consistency into the date as possible so that people can begin to plan their schedules around your servant evangelism events. Generally, The Journey holds their Servant Evangelism Saturdays on the second Saturday of every month.

Be sure to select the date at least three weeks in advance to allow for proper planning and scheduling time.

2. Decide upon a servant evangelism project at least two weeks in advance.

Select a specific project at least two weeks in advance of the date.

There are countless servant evangelism projects that your church can participate in. Things to consider when deciding upon a servant evangelism project include:

- How many people you plan on involving
- Quality vs. quantity of servant evangelism touch

Every time someone benefits or receives an act of service, this is considered a servant evangelism "touch."

How deeply you serve someone often affects the number of people you are able to serve. However, a deeper touch, by definition, makes a longer lasting impact upon an individual and may make the fewer touches worthwhile. Therefore, over the long run, it is important to achieve a balance between quality and quantity.

Other points to consider as you choose a project:

- What time of year is it? Are there seasonal projects to consider?
- What is the weather typically like this time of year?
- How much money are you willing to spend per touch? In total?
- Are you trying to reach a particular demographic?
- How will you purchase the supplies?
- How will you transport the supplies?

Remember, evangelism is an investment in the future, not an expense!

Participants are often willing to donate $10 to the project to provide for supplies if necessary.

3. Select the location for your Servant Evangelism Saturday at least two weeks in advance.

Select the location at least two weeks prior to the event. This will allow you adequate time to inform everyone of the location of the project before the event.

Choose an area with a high amount of local traffic. Avoid locations with high numbers of tourists or nonresidents, as they will not be able to respond to your servant evangelism project by attending your church.

Make sure the project that you have chosen will work well in the location that you choose. Will the typical demographic in the area appreciate the type of service you plan on doing? Make sure the project is conducted in a location that contains a high amount of traffic in your target demographic. The location you choose should have people who match your church culture. (Note: If the location and project are not a match, then one or the other must change. Everything should center on the people you are trying to reach. Never sacrifice the goal of your project—reaching people for Jesus and involving them in your church—for a specific location or servant evangelism project.)

4. Mobilize volunteers to serve during your Servant Evangelism Saturday.

The Journey mobilizes volunteers to serve at Servant Evangelism Saturdays through the following four ways:

Small groups: At the start of each semester, every small group is assigned a Servant Evangelism Saturday for that semester.

Servant Evangelism Saturdays are open to anyone who wants to participate; however, to ensure strong participation from the church's attenders, small groups are all asked to attend one Servant Evangelism Saturday per semester.

Two weeks before their scheduled servant evangelism project, the groups should be reminded about their scheduled SE date via email.

One week prior to their scheduled SE date, the leaders of each small group should receive a phone call reminding them about that Saturday's servant evangelism project.

In addition, one week prior, the servant evangelism leader for your church should email the assigned attendees directly to remind them about the upcoming SE event.

Each group will need to respond to you with an estimated attendance from their small group. This will enable you to better plan for servant evangelism supplies at the project.

Sunday flier: Beginning two Sundays before the Servant Evangelism Saturday, The Journey places a flier in the program for the upcoming event. This flier provides the time, location, date, and contact information for the SE Saturday.

Those who are interested in attending are encouraged to email a specific representative, who will be able to use this number to plan out how many servant evangelism supplies to provide.

Newsletter: This is a weekly email newsletter sent out to your church's database containing information on upcoming events at your church. A brief overview of the Servant Evangelism Saturday should be included here for the two weeks preceding the event. Those who are interested in attending are encouraged to email a specific representative. Here's an example of a newsletter announcement:

Servant Evangelism Saturday

Want to make a real difference in someone's day? Then join us Saturday afternoon on October 16 for Servant Evangelism Saturday! Servant Evangelism is a fun, easy, and meaningful way to share the love and message of Jesus through acts of service. For more information, email _____.

Website: The church's website should have a calendar that provides a brief description of the church's upcoming events. As soon as the date has been set for your servant evangelism project, this event should be placed on the website calendar. Example of brief description:

Servant Evangelism Saturday

Want to make a real difference in someone's day? Then join us Saturday afternoon, October 16, at 12:00 p.m. at Father Demo Square in the Village for Servant Evangelism Saturday! Servant Evangelism is a fun, easy, and meaningful way to share the love and message of Jesus through acts of service. For more information or to RSVP, please email _____.

Additional Pre-Event Preparation

The supplies for your event must be purchased and prepared to be used at your SE Saturday. Where you purchase the supplies and what preparation is required to get ready for the event is entirely dependent upon which project you have chosen. Depending on the project, The Journey has found great success with local warehouse stores such as BJ's or Sam's Club.

With each project, printed material must also be included. For example, if you are giving away water in a park on a hot summer day, each recipient must receive a bottle of water and a card about the church. The card about the church is often the only communication you are able to have with the recipient, so it is important that you include all the information about your church that they need to know. This information should include:

- service times and locations
- message series information—title of the series, titles of the Sunday messages and their corresponding dates
- church website

On Servant Evangelism Saturday

Before the event starts, all necessary supplies and printed material must be transported to the site and prepared as much as possible for the participants.

Get the event started approximately five to seven minutes after the planned start of the project:

1. Welcome everyone and thank them for coming.
2. Conduct a brief, five-minute training on servant evangelism.
   a. Define servant evangelism.
   b. Share some basic examples of SE (perhaps past projects, etc.).
   c. Briefly explain the biblical basis for it.
   d. Explain the impact that it has already had at your church and how God has been using it. Oftentimes people do

not understand how powerful a tool servant evangelism truly is. Explaining the impact servant evangelism has had at your church can truly motivate people.

3. Walk them through the key points on your church's card.

   a. Service times and locations

   b. Message information and dates

   c. Website

4. Conduct an overview of the project you will be doing that day.

   a. Explain the project. For example, if you are going to be giving away free bottles of water, explain what that means, etc.

   b. Explain the team structure for the project. In other words, how are you going to organize the volunteers? Let them know if they will be going out with a group of two, three, four, etc.

   c. Explain to them what to say as you do the project. Depending on the project, servant evangelism can be as simple as saying "Would you like a free granola bar?" If asked why, respond: "We just wanted to show you God's love in a practical way."

   Remind them that if they are asked a question they do not know the answer to, they should not make something up. They can direct the person to the church website or apologize for not knowing the answer but offer to put them in touch with someone who does at a Sunday service.

   d. Remind them to hand every recipient of the service a church card as well.

195

   e. Tell them to smile!

   f. Encourage them to pray throughout the event.

5. Answer any questions that they might have.
6. Announce a time to meet back after the project. Most projects work well if they last approximately sixty to ninety minutes.
7. Pray.
8. Divide the group into teams.
9. Distribute supplies and let the teams serve.

Throughout the event, be on the lookout for potential servant evangelism leaders for your church. Provide on-the-spot feedback to these leaders so that they can develop their servant evangelism skills.

Post-Event Wrap-Up

When the allotted time is up, wrap up the project:

- Collect leftover materials (postcards, servant evangelism supplies, etc.).
- Ask everyone how it went.
- Provide an opportunity for people to briefly share some stories.
- Answer any questions they may have.
- Remind them once again of the importance of what they did today.
- Thank them for coming and let them know when the next Servant Evangelism Saturday will be.
- Pray and close.

- Clean up after the event (pick up any cards on the sidewalk, etc.).
- Return supplies, equipment, leftover materials, etc.
- Count the number of touches.

Going Forward

To the best of your ability, track the number of first-time guests who attend your church in the weeks after the project that can be attributed to that Servant Evangelism Saturday.

Save those statistics to share with your SE participants in the future. Don't underestimate the ability of numbers of changed lives to inspire people!

If possible, contact everyone who participated and thank them once again for coming. Go ahead and remind them of the next project date.

Start developing key servant evangelism leaders. Have them read books, visit websites, and so on to expand their knowledge. I recommend:

- *Conspiracy of Kindness* by Steve Sjogren, considered the textbook on servant evangelism, and his website at www.servantevangelism.com
- www.ChurchLeaderInsights.com (my site for church leaders)
- *Irresistible Evangelism* by Steve Sjogren

To download this strategy, visit www.ignitebook.com.

appendix 6

new believer email

Subject: The Journey—Beginning a Relationship
From: Pastor Nelson Searcy

Hi [First Name],

On Sunday you indicated on your Connection Card that you were interested in knowing about becoming a follower of Jesus, and I wanted to let you know how excited I am for you! Becoming a follower of Jesus is one of the most important decisions you can make with your life.

I want to encourage and help you in any way that I can, so please let me know if you have any questions or if there is anything I can do for you. In fact, here are some important next steps you can take this week.

1. You can stop by our resource table on Sunday and pick up a New Believer Bible for free.
2. Baptism—Much like a wedding ring is symbolic of marital commitment, baptism is a symbolic act of your new relationship with Jesus. We encourage you to be baptized; it is an important next step for you!

   Our next baptism will be on [date] from 7:00–9:00 p.m. Check out http://www.journeymetro.com/resources/baptism for more information, or just reply to this email to sign up.
3. Serving is a great way to get connected! Not only is it a great way to meet new people, but it is also an opportunity to impact hundreds of people. You can serve on an upcoming Sunday or even during the week at our office. To sign up visit http://www.journeymetro.com/resources/serving_at_the_journey.

Again, I am so excited about your decision to begin a personal relationship with Jesus, and I want to help you follow through with this in any way that I can.

Blessings,
Pastor Nelson

P.S.: If you would like to speak with someone, please feel free to give us a call at (212) 730-8300 ext. 212, or reply to this email with your phone number and one of our pastors will be glad to give you a call.

new believer letter

Hello [Name],

On Sunday you indicated on your Connection Card that you were interested in knowing how to begin a relationship with Jesus. Becoming a follower of Jesus is the most important decision you can make in your life. I wanted to let you know how excited I am for you!

I have included a book for you that will help you begin your relationship with Christ on a solid foundation. I also included a DVD titled "What Does It Mean to Be a Christian?" to help you understand what your decision means and how it will change your life! A New Believer's Bible certificate is also enclosed in this letter. Please take the certificate to the resource table to receive your free new Bible.

The next step is for you to be baptized! Baptism is an important step for every believer. If you haven't been baptized, join The Journey on Friday, [date], from 7:00–9:00 p.m. for our Friday Night Baptism. We'll even have a special worship concert before the baptism! For more information on baptism, email Pastor Kerrick or visit: www.journeymetro.com/resources/baptism.

Again, I am so excited about your decision to begin a personal relationship with Jesus and want to help you follow through with this in any way that I can. Please give me a call at 212-730-8300 ext. 212 if you have any questions or would like to talk about your decision!

God bless . . .

Nelson Searcy
Lead Pastor, The Journey Church

P.S.: This Sunday we'll continue our new fall teaching series, Financial Peace, with "How Do I Manage Wealth?" We hope to see you there!

notes

Introduction

1. Rick Warren, *The Purpose-Driven Church* (Grand Rapids: Zondervan, 1995), 131.
2. Lausanne Committee for World Evangelisation, www.lausanne.org.
3. Jim Collins, *Built to Last* (New York: HarperCollins, 1997).

Chapter 4: Reaching the Boiling Point

1. Jim Collins, *Good to Great* (New York: HarperCollins, 2001), 85–86.

Chapter 7: Mobilizing for Evangelism

1. Peter Wagner, *Church Growth: State of the Art* (Carol Stream, IL: Tyndale, 1986), 53.
2. Stephen Covey, *The Seven Habits of Highly Effective People* (New York: Simon and Schuster, 2004), 151.

Chapter 9: Finding Fertile Ground

1. Warren, *Purpose-Driven Church*, 175.

Chapter 10: Sowing the Best Seed

1. Warren, *Purpose-Driven Church*, 196.